Praise for the

"The 5 Laws sets you up to win, teaching you to how to be better, break negative patterns, and build upward momentum. Your behaviors indeed predict your future, and the inside-out approach of Brett's work will put you on the path to success."
— **Stephen M. R. Covey**, author of
The New York Times bestseller *The Speed of Trust*

"Brett has an uncanny ability to connect people's behaviors to their results. The 5 laws book offers incredible insights into why people succeed and fail. What's more, it provides practical ways to accelerate success."
— **William F. Farley**, CEO, *Zrii*, Former CEO, *Fruit of the Loom*

"Success is predictable — IF you know the five laws that determine it. Get this book and learn them, live them, and profit from them — NOW."
— **Dr. Joe Vitale**, author *The Attractor Factor* www.mrfire.com

"Brett Harward's *The 5 Laws* is a must read for anyone who is bored of the average and ordinary. Not only does he give examples of how to achieve success, he teaches the successful to have more success. I would sum up *The 5 Laws* in these five words: Brilliant, insightful, inspiring, direct and powerful."
— **Kirk Harpole**, President, *AllMakes Masonry, Inc.*

"As an executive working with dental providers around the country, I immediately saw the practical impact of the 5 Laws not only on my business, but all of those with whom I work. This book is full of insights that bring clarity to a working environment where any practitioner would experience immediate personal and financial results."
— **Andrew Eberhardt**, Vice President, *Dental Patient Care America*

"Brett's insights into life and business are remarkable to me. Each time I implement something I've learned from him it completely transforms the thing I'm doing and makes it easier, more pleasant and more satisfying to everyone involved. The principles in this book are changing my life — and making it better in every way."
— **Brenton M. Ripley**, Attorney At Law

"I have had the great fortune to not only read Brett Harward's new book, *The 5 Laws*, but also experience Brett's personal training expertise. Both on the page and in person, Brett is one of those rare individuals who actually walks his talk. *The 5 Laws* is filled with real life examples of how these laws that Brett has gleaned over his many years as a business owner, personal development trainer and business coach, are at the core of what creates success in life, not just monetary but emotional as well. This is a must read at this time of such great change on our planet!"

—**Steven Wand**, co-author of
Living the HeartLife... Letting Go of the Hard Life

"Brett is a brilliant teacher and coach. His ideas are insightful, funny and out of the box. I laughed throughout much of the book as I saw myself doing exactly what he talks about in his examples. What's best is that you'll see life positively different as soon as you read this book."

—**Mike Petroff**, Senior Enterprise Account Executive, *Omniture*

"My business and profits have grown by leaps and bounds since I've started applying Brett's ideas in my business and how I deal with others. He has practical and usable insights that don't get caught up in just theory."

—**Alan Johnson**, President, *IMS*

"Brett walked into my business 4 years ago making big promises... and he did exactly what he said he would do. Best business experience I've ever had. A couple years later my wife and I attended one of his personal development workshops. WOW!!! The insights he shares in the 5 Laws work."

—**Shawn Atkinson**, President, *AKI Industries*

"Brett steps into our training room each month for our non-profit organization and keeps everyone in the room riveted from his words on. His style is blunt, honest and hard-hitting. I see the miracle firsthand that occurs when others are presented with different choices when they are stuck in life. Hooray for finally writing a book, Brett."

—**Pamela Orvis**, Executive Director, **The Great Life Foundation**

"Brett Harward's common sense approach to the basic laws for success is refreshing, insightful, and provocative. The principles are simple and yet powerful. *The 5 Laws* is a must read for anyone looking to excel in business and in life."

—**McKinley Oswald**, Owner, *Sound Concepts*

"Brett possesses many gifts including the rare ability to look deep into individuals and companies and see patterns that determine outcomes. Brett also possesses an uncanny gift of teaching others to look inward at themselves or their companies to determine those patterns and in this book he gives you the tools to change those patterns if needed to effect your outcomes. I have witnessed first-hand the transformation of people and companies when putting into practice the important principles taught in this insightful book. I highly recommend it."

—**Randy Larsen**, Co-founder, *MonaVie*

"This book is excellent! The principles are fresh and not just fluff. The financial professionals we work with would be well served by the principles taught in the 5 laws."

—**Lyn Fisher**, CEO, *Financial Forum, Inc*

"I had no idea what I was walking into a year and a half ago when I walked into one of Brett's courses. My wife and I both attended and I was skeptical. Brett cut right to the chase. We learned entirely new ways to communicate with each other. It saved our marriage. Needless to say, we're big fans of his workshops and his book. What he says works."

—**Brandon Pehrson**, Real Estate Developer

"Brett Harward's book on the 5 laws is fantastic!! It brings simple, yet profound natural principles to your daily life which is the framework of how to truly go from surviving in life to thriving and succeeding. I love the metaphorical stories to bring the laws to light, and the personal touchstones he refers to in his own journey. Brett walks his talk and is a powerful advertisement for his own message, as he thrives and succeeds in his life on every level, and is deeply committed to providing the way for others to do the same. Thank you Brett for finally sharing your wisdom in a book, what a gift this is to the world!"

—**Cynthia Wand**, Co-Author of
Living the HeartLife ... Letting go of the Hard Life

"I've had other coaches, but never dreamed I'd be where I'm at today ... until Brett taught me about vision and frequency. He's been a key advisor both from a business and personal standpoint and I trust his insights explicitly. I would not be experiencing my levels of success without him"

—**Jim Weddington**, *JP Electric*

THE 5 LAWS

THAT DETERMINE

ALL OF LIFE'S

OUTCOMES

THE **5** LAWS

THAT DETERMINE

ALL OF LIFE'S

OUTCOMES

by Brett Harward

Acknowledgements

This book is a collaborative effort to say the least. Even though my father is no longer with us, he showed me there is a different way to treat others. Jayson Orvis challenged every assertion I made and contributed greatly to the thoughts and ideas presented in this book. My business partners Chad, Julie, Jerry, Natalie, Bayandor and Sandra have contributed enormously to my life and allowed me to be a total flake while I've worked on this book. Thank you to my friends Mike, Lanny and Tracy who read version after version of this manuscript. I also appreciate the numerous clients and family members who have read and contributed their insights and have given their time generously. Kim Simpson served as my editor and attempted to keep me politically correct. Thank you to each of you. I wouldn't have finished without you.

Contents

Foreword — *by Joel Martin*   xiii

Preface   xv

Prologue   1

Chapter 1 — *What Are The 5 Laws?*   9

SECTION 1

The First Law: The Law of Vision

Chapter 2 — *The Law of Vision (Know Your Target)*   15

Chapter 3 — *Vision Is The Key That Unlocks Depth*   25

Chapter 4 — *Vision Provides Direction*   31

Chapter 5 — *Vision-driven Communication*   39

SECTION 2

The Second Law: The Law of Frequency

Chapter 6 — *The Law of Frequency (Adapt Quickly)*   47

Chapter 7 — *The Monkey's Dilemma*   53

Chapter 8 — *The Need to Be Right Brings Frequency to a Screeching Halt*   59

Chapter 9 — *7 Steps to Achieve a Faster Frequency in Life*   65

SECTION 3

The Third Law: The Law of Perception

Chapter 10 — *The Law of Perception (Feedback)*   83

Chapter 11 — *Refraction*   91

Chapter 12 — *Be Willing to Be Wrong*   95

Chapter 13 — *Value Drivers*   101

Chapter 14 — *How Do We Tap into Other People's Value Drivers and Perceptions?*   107

Chapter 15 — *Value Quotient*   111

SECTION 4

The Fourth Law: The Law of Accountability

Chapter 16 — *The Law of Accountability (Ownership)*   125

Chapter 17 — *Account for Our Contribution to an Outcome*   131

Chapter 18 — *Reduce Drag*   137

Chapter 19 — *Three Tools to Reduce the Secondary Conversation with Other People Through Accountability*   143

SECTION 5

The Fifth Law: The Law of Leadership

Chapter 20 — *The Law of Leadership (Harness the IQ of Others)*   153

Chapter 21 — *The Human Dilemma*   159

Chapter 22 — *Creating an Effective Brain Trust*   163

Chapter 23 — *The Power of Aggregating IQ*   167

Chapter 24 — *Six Indicators of Potential IQ Points*   171

Chapter 25 — *Applying the 5 Laws: Newton's Second Law of Motion*   177

Epilogue   187

Foreword

APPROXIMATELY TWO YEARS AGO, I had the distinct honor of meeting Brett Harward, the author of *The 5 Laws That Determine All of Life's Outcomes*. At the time, Brett was (and still is) a successful business coach, business owner, family man, and humanitarian. I had been hired to "step in" to deliver a program for The Great Life Foundation in Salt Lake City. I knew that I could facilitate the breakthroughs their attendees were hungry to have in order to propel their lives, careers, relationships, and communities to a higher level. I knew that the Great Life grads would place these trainings among the top five experiences of their lives as my previous graduates had done. I knew that with my 20-plus years as an international trainer and coach I could make a contribution to the city. However, what I did not know—and came as a wonderful surprise to me—was that waiting in the training room along with about 50 participants was a man that I would soon be calling my friend, fellow visionary in changing the world, partner, and new lead transformational trainer.

I've led trainings and worked with professionals in South Africa, France, the United Kingdom, Latvia, Finland, Malaysia, Russia, and China. I'm driven by my love of people and commitment to their success. So when Brett told me that in addition to everything else he was up to in his already busy life, he wanted to lead transformational trainings, I agreed, of course. And "the rest is history," as the expression goes.

Brett has an extraordinary gift for clarity, seeing the best in others, telling a story, and providing hard-hitting solutions as well as dependable personal tools. I've seen him in action where he's been a no-holds-barred coach—entertaining, bold, and inspirational in one moment and a relentless "heat-seeking missile" busting up mediocrity in the next. While this book is no substitute for attending one of his keynotes or participating in a transformational training that he leads, it promises to give you the essence of his unique philosophy.

His book follows in the tradition of the best business books that I've read. It will be clear to you as you read *The 5 Laws That Determine All of Life's Outcomes* that here is a set of tools that have worked for thousands of businesses and individuals. Follow the chapters, use the 5 Laws and practice the counsel that Brett offers. Your business, organization, family, and community will benefit. He has skillfully blended quantum physics and the laws of nature with the laws that govern the heart. He's provided a step-by-step formula for success. He has included real-life examples of what happens when the 5 Laws are not applied effectively and examples of what's possible when they are.

I also appreciate his ability to connect the laws of nature and science with business and life accomplishment. Absorb the contents of this book and you will, as sure as the tried, tested, and true law of gravity, be a beneficiary of the brilliance of Brett Harward. His training, coaching, and consulting experience are behind his words—he knows what he's talking about. There is no hot air or fluff inside. He lives the 5 Laws and he is honest enough to share the times when he has not.

I agree with his philosophy that "the language of business is a universal language that transcends politics, religion, race, gender, and cultural boundaries. Together, if we transform our businesses, we can transform the world." For this reason, I wholeheartedly endorse *The 5 Laws That Determine All of Life's Outcomes* and recommend it to all readers who are interested in the transformation of their businesses and lives, because it's a book about the kind of success that we can predict.

My wish for you is that you will read on and start improving your business, careers and life today. With the 5 Laws in action we can transform the world.

Joel Martin, Ph.D.
President, Triad West Inc.
Author, *"How To Be A Positively Powerful Person"*
Mentor

Preface

SUCCESS IS PREDICTABLE. As a business owner, professional speaker, facilitator, and business coach, I've had opportunities to work with a wide variety of people, observing how they behave and giving much thought to the attributes of success and mediocrity. I've learned from the über-successful, as my friend Tracy would say, as well as the über-unsuccessful. (Apparently, according to her, "über" on the front of any word means ultra or super.) I work with many of the business elite as well as individuals who have been recommended or sentenced by the courts to attend workshops I have facilitated. Many times I have both types of people in the same room where I can contrast their behaviors and beliefs in the exact same context.

Above all, I've noticed the predictability of patterns people follow in their lives. A pattern is a way of framing life based on a belief that causes a person to behave in certain ways on a regular basis. People follow patterns of success, failure, and mediocrity in their finances, relationships, and all other areas of life. These patterns eventually become more predictive of success than our education, opportunity or luck. You probably know of men or women who seem to turn everything they touch into gold from a financial perspective. Perhaps more common are those who, no matter what they do, struggle financially. Some people have deep, meaningful relationships with almost everyone they associate and interact with. Others have patterns that foster a lack of trust and result in troubled, shallow relationships once again with almost everyone. Some patterns foster growth, learning, and success, and others foster setbacks, sabotage, and frustration. We like to think that success or even failure are a matter of stars aligning or not aligning. Our fate instead is written on the tablets of our heart, or the troubled waters of our ego.

There are three factors that make it difficult for us to recognize and learn from our own patterns. The first of these is the time disconnect that usually occurs between our patterns and our results. Often, years separate the initial pattern activities and the end result. This separation causes people to not connect the two. For example, a small business owner who doesn't watch his or her numbers is likely to survive for some time. In the end, that pattern of not paying attention to the numbers will run the business into the ground. Likewise, someone who has a pattern of being a poor listener will eventually struggle with relationships even if it takes awhile for the relationship to suffer the corresponding meltdown that comes from not listening.

The second factor is the reality that the true impact of a given pattern is clearest in the long term. Patterns can be predictive of short-term results, although they only guarantee results over long periods. Because people sometimes experience short-term successes or failures that don't seem to align with the patterns they have developed, they can have difficulty connecting their long-term results with those same patterns. It's like "hitting" a 20 in blackjack. Every now and then you will get an ace and end up with a perfect 21. A pattern of hitting a 20, though, will guarantee a "blackjack disaster" in the long run.

The final reason that our patterns are so hard to see is that our negative patterns are the last thing in the world that we want to see. We want to see ourselves as good, smart, kind, successful, fill in the adjective. Because of that we don't like to look at areas that might indicate otherwise. It is much easier to see our approach or response in life as the best approach, the only approach, or the reasonable approach discounting results that are less than impressive that come from our typical patterns. Usually, despite experiencing similar results from a series of different circumstances we fail to see that we are the common denominator, not the other people.

Let me repeat: Most people never make the connection between their patterns in life and the outcomes they experience. They see results as a simple game of chance where they win some and lose some. They exaggerate their wins and minimize their losses so that the patterns and behaviors never change. They see themselves as being much closer to success than they actually are, and blame people and conditions outside of their control for their shortfalls and issues. Some have mastered the self-help lingo and jargon, read the books, and speak in terms of accountability and ownership without any substantial shift in results. Some have achieved high results in some areas of their lives while struggling in other areas. And others fixate on areas where results are difficult if not impossible to measure, such as spirituality or "being a good person."

The game of blackjack, again, is a particularly good illustration of some of the ways that life, too, can be played. In this game, a player typically gives up a very slight advantage to the house. The actual numbers vary slightly depending on the rules of any individual game, but a good player can generally win over 49% of the time with the house winning just over 50% of the time. Poor players face much lower odds, while world-class players who count cards and are willing to follow strict rules of discipline can actually get a slight advantage over the house. The average clueless player makes too many mistakes to even come close to breaking even with the house and is therefore, over time, guaranteed to lose before even playing the game. I've seen players make decisions without even looking at their own cards even though they're entitled to this advantage in any blackjack game. Probabilities of winning are almost entirely dependent on what cards you see. World-class blackjack players win because they are acutely aware of every possible card that is in play as well as what's out of play. Imagine how much more effective you would be at blackjack if you knew every card that everyone had including you and the dealer. Although you wouldn't win every hand, common sense would ensure that you would win the majority. How much more would you be willing to bet knowing that the odds were in your favor?

This book is about developing the patterns and behaviors that promote success over the long term. For most people, this approach will dramatically improve short-term success as well. It will, in fact, be like playing life with all the cards face up. The approach incorporates five laws that determine all of life's outcomes. Everyone uses these laws in some form or another. The laws govern without respect, much like the law of gravity.

Gravity—when combined with other principles or laws of physics such as thrust and resistance—becomes part of the equation for flying jet airliners. When the laws of physics are used optimally for jet airline flight they will lift a 200 ton aircraft into the stratosphere. Gravity is especially critical for a successful landing. By the same token, that law can prove catastrophic for airplane flight when applied poorly. The law of gravity applies whether we use it to land a plane or crash a plane. It is consistent and it doesn't change, show favoritism, or apply itself based on morality or judgment.

I have a vision of a planet where war is no longer an option in resolving conflict, and I am committed to playing whatever role I can in making that happen. From my perspective, much of human conflict, if not all, centers on the frustrations, disappointments and war within the individual human heart. So many of us, being only human, focus much of our lives on mere survival, which restricts us to instant, self-serving, and shortsighted solutions that overlook issues of wider impact or long-term sustainability. I refer to this as the difference between a "surviving consciousness" and a "thriving consciousness." It's high time we mastered that latter option. This book addresses the 5 Laws that can move us in that direction.

Prologue

THE DROUGHT THAT WAS RAVAGING the savannas of Uganda was in its 10th season. The earth had become parched and cracked like the hands of a weather-beaten old man. Miko's tribe had fared better than most, but it now stood at the gates of extinction. A hunter, he was far older than most of the others, who were typically the youngest and strongest members of the tribe. He had lived many seasons and had become revered as "The Great Hunter." However, over the last 10 seasons, the area his tribe inhabited had fallen into the throes of the worst drought that he had ever experienced. While many of the surrounding tribes had suffered the death of many of their children due to a lack of food and water in a land once abundant with game, others were brought to extinction. Miko's tribe had taken in a number of the scattered survivors of these ill-fated tribes, accepting them as their own. Now, though, even with the advantage of being great hunters, Miko's tribe faced obliteration because the game had become so depleted.

In his youth, Miko had established himself as a great hunter. His father had been a great hunter, and Miko followed closely in his father's footsteps. As a young boy he had played hunting games with the other boys. He dreamed about the day that he would be able to hunt large game on his own. He saw any stick that was lying on the ground as a spear, and would often attempt to craft a weapon from resources he scavenged from the area where the tribe was currently camping. The tribe moved regularly to follow the patterns of the animals and the water.

As Miko grew older he was brought along more frequently on hunting trips with his father and the older children. Although he was still only a child, he felt the weight of his tribe's high expectations and their reliance on his ability to provide sustenance. He also loved the challenge, thrill, and honor of the hunt. Much of his early success came from trial and error. With abundant game, mistakes and misses were easy to tolerate, and the tribe rarely had to experience the pangs of hunger from lack of food. Because the sweltering heat of his homeland made the long-term preservation of meat a near impossibility, hunting was an essential, daily activity.

As critical as the hunt was for the survival of the tribe, only a small group of men were charged with the task. Being a hunter rivaled any of the other leadership positions, and the largest and strongest young men in the tribe usually selected themselves as the hunters. After all, while it was one thing to get close enough to an animal to aim a spear at it, it was quite another to summon enough strength to propel the spear through the tough hides of the animals. Many a good throw simply bounced off of the zebra, buffalo, gazelle or other savanna animal, after which they would gallop out of range. Miko hated those moments, and vowed to throw even harder at his next opportunity.

Most of the time, however, his throws simply missed their intended target. Or even worse, his throws would hit and penetrate the animal's hide, but would not hit in a vital area. Miko was raised with a reverence and respect for the animals he hunted. Wounding an animal and causing it to suffer brought him great discomfort and sleepless nights. The suffering he brought to animals that were wounded as a result of his lack of skill prompted Miko to start traveling down a hunting path that was quite different from those of his tribesmen.

For generations the other hunters had accepted the fact that although skill was definitely a factor in hunting, there was nonetheless much out of the hunter's control, based as it was on trial and error. The best hunters became excellent at estimating distances, throwing speeds and trajectory and could direct their spears with reasonable accuracy. Miko had fallen into that category, seeing that most of the other hunters, including him for a time, drew a false sense of satisfaction from the near misses. They regaled their families with the stories of the great hunt that ended with a near miss. Children would sit at the feet of the hunters listening as they tried to ignore their hunger pangs. Most of the hunters just hunted harder to accommodate their misses. But this was often problematic because they would find themselves exhausted and unprepared when opportunities presented themselves. Much of the time they failed to even make adjustments to their throws or equipment, instead blaming the wind, the animal, or some other aspect of the hunt that was out of their control. Consequently, they made the same mistakes frequently. With the abundance of game this teaching was never questioned. However, the misses were too frequent and too painful for Miko. He knew he was missing something elemental in his approach.

That's when Miko became a student of the laws of hunting and spears. He'd been taught, like the others in his tribe, to spend little time making his spears and weapons. Too many tribesmen had spent considerable time on a spear at some point only to have it run off with a wounded animal. Better to make them disposable, was the general thought. When game was plentiful, that thought and strategy produced acceptable results. Miko, however, took the time to make sure each spear he used had the capacity for penetration if he were to hit his mark. He recognized that he needed to spend at least the same amount of time he used for honing his spear for learning how to make himself effective at hitting the target. He recognized that in earlier years he had thrown many a spear that had been poorly made and was altogether incapable of penetrating the thick hide of the game he was pursuing. Never again, he promised himself.

Miko also saw the importance of accurate measurements in a successful hunt and developed the skill to be extremely effective at estimating distances. He would regularly guess at the distance of a bush or tree and then count off the paces to see how close he was. He could always guess within one or two paces. Now, he was seeing that being off by one or two paces was often the difference between a quick kill and wounding an animal. He explored various methods of improving his accuracy and eventually found some that improved his results measurably.

As he killed game, he even took time to explore the insides of the animals he killed. He took note of some of the vital organs that, when hit, would produce the fastest and cleanest kill. Likewise, he noted organs and areas on the animals that produced slower death or only injury so that he could avoid those areas. And he noticed that different kinds of animals had slightly different vital areas.

Miko also studied how length, diameter, weight and material affected how far and straight his spears flew. He made sure to select stones for spearheads that were the same size so he could improve his chances for accuracy. Miko wasn't alone in recognizing most of the factors that led to a successful hunt. To some degree all the hunters had learned the general parameters that Miko was recognizing and applied them loosely on an intuitive level. Miko, however, went much deeper. He was amazed at the consistency with which each of these variables produced results after he understood how they worked. He discovered that there was absolutely nothing random about the trajectory of a spear, and that a miss of any degree wasn't due to poor luck, but rather failure to apply or account for some predictable and measurable law.

He spent much of his time dropping rocks and spears, pacing, watching the flight paths, and exploring the anatomy of the animals he hunted. He started noticing that even the smallest outside factors like wind, rain, humidity and altitude each played a predictable role in the flight of his spear. While he might not have been able to fully explain some of these influences, there was always enough information at his disposal to give him insights and messages about how these factors would affect his throw. Eventually, the same factors that had at one time thwarted his ability to hunt successfully became reliable allies for Miko and his spear. Because of his accuracy, Miko was able to spend far less time hunting than other tribesmen. On his rare misses, he always went back through what had happened to determine what factors he had failed to account for. He also learned from each of his successful throws. After all, he knew that the result he had achieved was predictable.

Now, years later, Miko had established his own set of rules or laws that he knew governed the flight of his spear and the success of his hunt. He had broken them down to 5 specific areas or laws:

1. **Know your target.** Know exactly what the objective is. Miko had conducted many a hunt in his own mind. He could describe exactly where

his target was with each animal he hunted. He saw the path of the spear in his mind before making any throw. In seeing the path of the spear, he also saw any twigs, blades of grass, or other obstacles that would impact the spear's trajectory. By anticipating those issues he was able to make adjustments to his throw or angle that would provide a clear flight trajectory for his spear.

2. **Learn quickly.** Without constant experimentation, Miko couldn't have possibly learned how each condition affected the flight of his spear. He always tested his assumptions before applying them in the hunt. He embraced failure as an opportunity to see an unaccounted-for condition. He found that failure fueled innovation when he maintained focus on the target. He learned how to correct ineffective aspects of his throw and rid himself of any equipment that didn't produce his desired results.

3. **Listen and observe.** Miko knew that there were many things that affected a spear's flight. Some of them were difficult to see by himself. He couldn't see the wind or humidity, but the grass and tree branches could provide clues on how these might affect his throw. Often, he would be the last one to see approaching game. But the birds and other animals had better vantage points, and when he listened to them and observed them, he was better prepared. He knew that the sounds and noises of the savanna, including silence, could warn him of approaching danger or food. The plant life and terrain also provided accurate and readily available indicators of his altitude. Most hunters ignored such factors as random, calling them lucky or unlucky depending on the result of the throw. Some considered them to be too complex to attempt to solve, or they saw them as the result of some sort of divine providence acting beyond their own ability to understand. Miko found that he could always ask the grass, tree leaves, insects, birds or other animals and they would give him reliable answers about the outside conditions that would impact his throw.

4. **Own the results of each throw.** Only by owning—that is, taking full responsibility for—his misses and his hits was Miko able to improve his skill. He learned that if he focused on what he did or didn't do to create the result of each throw, he could adapt quickly, and he rarely made the

same mistake twice. Because he never blamed outside factors or other people or even chastised himself, he had opportunities to learn from each miss or success, therefore finding that he had much more control over his outcomes than he had once thought.

5. **Expand learning beyond yourself.** Ultimately, Miko's vision of the tribe's prosperity could only be fulfilled if Miko could share what he had learned among all of the tribe's hunters. Growing older and more frail, he knew a time would come when even he would have to rely on the abilities of those around him. Miko recognized the importance not only of teaching, but learning from the other hunters in the tribe. Miko's own commitment to learning and teaching could go a long way toward ensuring the success of the tribe's future. If he didn't expand the body of learning that existed in the tribe, all of his efforts would be for naught when he could no longer hunt. He knew that as he shared his learning and learned from others, that the collective knowledge of the tribe would increase and that his fellow tribesmen would all become better hunters. Thus, in Miko's tribe campfire stories evolved from bragging and storytelling to learning opportunities for young and old alike.

Now, with the drought on the verge of wiping out his tribe, the stakes were much higher. He knew that the survival of the tribe was on his shoulders. The tribe's food supply had dwindled to nothing. The children and adults were growing thinner by the day, including Miko's own children. Miko had not even seen any game for four entire days, much less gotten close enough to make an attempt with his spear. As was his custom, he had gotten up before the sun and traveled to one of the few watering holes within walking distance of where his tribe had set up camp.

This particular watering hole was one of Miko's favorites. His father had brought him here years ago on his first real hunting trip. When the tribe traveled he always looked forward to returning to this spot. The watering hole was easy to recognize because of the three giant, rectangle-shaped granite boulders that rose from the grassy savanna, each one taller than the last. From the base of the three stones sprang a small stream that fed the pond year round. Unlike the basin ponds that collected groundwater from surrounding hills and dried out during certain parts of the year, this small pond erupted from nowhere. It pooled up in the small depression in the ground and overflowed down the opposite side, forming a small stream no more than a finger's depth. The stream flowed for about twelve paces to the roots of a giant cypress tree before it almost magically disappeared back into the ground.

He began his methodical setup that had initially drawn laughs from the other hunters. But now he knew that other hunters from his tribe would be following the same ritual in the places where they were hunting. They had learned and shared as a group, and each was aware of the gravity of the day's hunt. He was alone today. It had been decided that because of the scarcity of game, the hunters would spread out and increase their chances of spotting an animal. He walked silently to the edge of the small spring-fed pond, and he began pacing. He bent a small reed in half at 20 paces and again at 30. His outer range was 40 paces and he bent one more piece of grass at that distance. The bent pieces of dry grass were barely perceptible even to him, but he knew his marks well. He continued pacing and marking from any angle that might afford him a shot. Now the light was starting to appear beyond the distant horizon.

Next, he picked up a small clump of dried grass from where he stood. As had become his custom, he dropped it from the exact same height he always had, and watched as the slight breeze blew it one-and-a-half paces as it fell to the ground. He hefted the spear, the same one he had used on his last 10 successful hunting trips. He rubbed a small nick on the spear with his calloused fingers to smooth it out. And then he sat silently.

The white birds that frequently bathed in the watering hole suddenly erupted in flight. Miko knew what that often meant, and his pulse quickened. Then he heard the animal approaching through the dry grass. A few seconds later, Miko's heart jumped as he saw the cautious wildebeest approaching the water along one of the trails he had been watching. The animal was wary as it approached the hole. Miko silently moved to his left where he could get a clean throw. There was a large bush ahead which made it so that the wildebeest couldn't see him approach. As he got closer he could see the back of the animal with its head down, drinking. He looked at the grass to his left and saw one of the bent pieces he had marked earlier. Exactly 40 paces. With each additional step he counted, 39, 38, 37. The Wildebeest suddenly looked up. It was getting nervous. Miko's heart stopped. "Please put your head down one more time," he whispered to himself. As he saw the animal's head once again drop below the grass he re-checked all of his variables. This was a long throw, and Miko had never made a throw with so much riding on it. As the spear left his hand, Miko knew that the outcome of the throw had already been determined. The laws now took effect. The breeze, gravity, spear, and speed all combined to create the only possible trajectory for his spear. Time seemed to go into slow motion as each of these so-called variables acted together to make their completely predictable impact on the spear's path.

The wildebeest caught some movement out of the corner of its eye, but it was too late. The spear struck deep, piercing the heart of the large animal. It ran less than 20 paces. Miko's tribe would be celebrating and eating tonight. Although Miko didn't know it at the time the parched savannas would soon return to the lush green that he had known as a child, in a few weeks the rain would start to fall. His tribe, his family, would thrive.

CHAPTER ONE

What are The 5 Laws?

T HE 5 LAWS DETERMINE THE PROBABILITY of success and of failure over time. They are extremely predictive of outcomes in relationships, finances, business, health, and personal fulfillment. Every one of us applies them continually, regardless of whether we are experiencing success or failure. It doesn't matter whether or not we know what the laws are and how they work. Rather than being a checklist of things to do, they represent *ways of being.* As you apply these 5 Laws they will bleed over into every area of your life, such as money, parenting, friendships, and romantic relationships. You will notice a fundamental shift in how you interact with others and how they perceive you. Best of all, you will see your self-defeating patterns reverse themselves, leveraging previous successes and building upward momentum.

When you observe them and adhere to them, the 5 Laws will create endlessly positive patterns in your life that will also ensure success in the long term. The natural result of adopting them in our lives is to see choices and options where most people miss them. And they govern our very abilities to tap into the depths of our human potential and success.

Here are the 5 Laws:

1. **The Law of Vision**—Governs depth and direction in human beings and is the foundational element of successfully applying the other laws. It demands an uncommon depth of commitment.

2. **The Law of Frequency**—Determines our rate of acceleration toward achieving our life objectives.

3. **The Law of Perception**—Expands our own insights when we readily incorporate the perceptions of others.

4. **The Law of Accountability**—Demands that we own our contributions to the results we experience. It allows us to experience being powerful and in control of our lives. This essentially equates to speed learning.

5. **The Law of Leadership**—Converts the sea of humanity that stands between you and your vision from adversaries to allies.

Many of us have probably found ourselves approaching life as though we were playing the classic carnival game "Whack-a-Mole." In this game, a player stands in front of a machine that has multiple holes. The player holds a mallet and when the game starts the player gets points whenever they can "whack" a plastic mole on the head with the soft mallet as it pops up momentarily through a random hole. As the player hits one mole on the head another one pops up elsewhere. Most players tend to play just a half a second behind the moles with their mallet regularly landing on an empty hole because the mole has already disappeared. Even if you hit one of the elusive targets it's sure to pop up again a few moments later. It can be an exhausting and frustrating game.

When we focus only on the short-term, our lives can feel very much like an endless game of Whack-a-Mole. We feel as though we're standing in one spot, constantly dealing with the same problems over and over again, never moving forward and learning little, if anything, new. "Why try harder?" we find ourselves asking. We may talk about higher ambitions, but the gap between what we say and the results we experience is like the Grand Canyon. Our own behaviors, habits and ways of being seem so deeply ingrained and impassible that crossing that gap to where we want to be seems almost impossible. Stay tuned, it is possible. To be sure, it's a journey and certainly isn't for the faint of heart. Most of us have a behavioral idiosyncrasy or two that others may consider peculiar or perhaps even annoying. Such "quirks" are not my concern, so much as the pathological behavioral flaws that prevent us from succeeding. Psychologists use the word "pathological" in the sense of "behavior that is habitual, maladaptive, and compulsive." Indeed, my usage of the term, "pathological behavior" throughout this book refers to an individual's repeated, habitual actions that conflict directly with that same individual's own best interests. These behaviors keep people from getting what they want out of life, and they often create downward spirals or self-fulfilling prophecies. Here are some examples of these types of downward spirals:

- A man has developed severe anger issues because he feels like he's been abandoned throughout his life. His anger and negativity continue to drive people away from him, thus reinforcing his anger.

- A woman who is bitter about a husband's infidelity pushes him and other men away because of her guarded, emotional disconnectedness and lack of trust. Feeling closed off, the men in her life are liable to seek more emotionally satisfying relationships elsewhere, thus fueling her bitterness and lack of trust.

- A manager who is passed over for a promotion that starts to resent coworkers, seeing them as competition and the reason for his not being promoted. This resentment leads to stifled communication and poor rapport with fellow team members. His increasingly obvious sense of disconnect from his work environment and lack of collegiality will likely guarantee that he will be passed over on future promotions, thereby fanning the flame of his resentment.

- A business owner is struggling financially and decides that he should spend as little as possible on employee wages and marketing expenses. He tightens down on these expenses, after which he loses good employees and his business growth stagnates even more. He interprets this as evidence that it's difficult to make profits and grow his business. He also seals his own fate as a business owner.

The purpose of this book is to help you see beyond the horizon, to help you move beyond Whack-a-Mole living, to avoid getting bogged down by negative, self-fulfilling prophecies, and to understand that your behavior predicts your future. The Laws outlined in this book will open your eyes to different choices and options in life. One of the most influential military strategy books of all-time is called *The Art of War*. It was written over 2,500 years ago by a Chinese general named Sun Tzu (pronounced "sun sue"). His book has been translated into many languages and hundreds of derivative books have drawn from his battle concepts. Today, his ideas are applied more often to business as well as interpersonal and group dynamics than to battle strategies. Perhaps Sun Tzu's most profound concept in his book is the one about predictability. He states that in every battle ever fought, the results are already determined prior to fighting the battle. In other words, the battle itself has less to do with its outcome than with the specific parameters that are already in place before the battle is fought. Similarly, the manner of our engagement in life is predictive of success or failure even before we commence with any specific activity. By knowing the 5 Laws and consciously integrating them into your daily habits, you too will be able to predict your success.

THE FIRST LAW

THE LAW OF

VISION

CHAPTER TWO

The Law of Vision (Know Your Target)

V ISION IS WHAT GIVES US THE POWER to initiate movement; it's also the force that acts upon us when we decide to change direction. Perhaps Sir Isaac Newton best described this with his first Law of Motion, otherwise known as Newton's Law. It states that objects at rest tend to stay at rest, while objects in motion tend to stay in motion at the same speed and direction, unless acted upon by an unbalanced force. This law applies equally to objects and people. Where people are concerned, Newton's law could be restated as follows: People that are stuck tend to stay stuck, while people who are in motion tend to stay in motion at the same speed and direction, unless acted upon by a vision.

Visions are not wishes, and the big difference between those has to do with one's level of engagement. For me, the term *vision* means far more than just setting goals—it's a driving force that's synonymous with purpose, commitment and passion. Vision serves two primary purposes: it engages the deepest parts of who we are and provides direction. Visions are separated from wishes, ideas, and goals by the depth of our engagement. By tapping our human depth, vision causes us to extend ourselves well beyond that level which we would normally engage (our comfort zone).

Last year I went on an evening fly-fishing trip with four friends. We had been talking about getting out on a local river for several months and one day we finally decided that we would get going that very afternoon. I packed a good bit of gear in the back of my car before I left, and picked up some flies to add to the ones I had been tying for the previous several days. We agreed to a meeting time and place a few hours away, and all four of us arrived within minutes of each other. Each of us had done considerable fishing in our day, or could at least talk a good "fishing game." The rest of our little group followed me to a parking spot that was only a few yards away from a steep bank that went twenty yards down to the river. We each opened up our car trunks and started gearing up, putting on our waders and setting up our fly rods. It was late in the afternoon so we were in somewhat of a hurry to get on the water. That's when I noticed that one of the four of us was just standing around. I asked him why he wasn't putting on his waders.

He explained that he didn't really have time to get his gear together for the trip that day but that he'd be happy to watch us fish. Fortunately, I had brought extra waders, extra rods and reels, and other assorted gear that he might need. Reluctantly he agreed to gear up as the rest of us anxiously waited for him to get ready. I tied some flies onto the line of the rod I was loaning him as he put on his waders. Finally, he was ready to go. As we approached the bank that led to the river, our reluctant fisherman decided he would watch for a while. He pointed to riffles and rocks in the river and told the rest of us that that is where we would likely catch fish. The rest of us couldn't wait any longer, so we plowed down the bank into the cold, clear water and began navigating the river.

Another one of our group decided to start fishing the area right next to the parking lot. Two of us decided to head downstream to waters that had been fished less frequently. Because we only had a few hours to fish, we hiked quickly along the bank and through the brush to find a good spot downstream. After hiking for about a mile we came across a long deep hole where the small river cut into the bank on the far side. The far bank was overgrown with trees and shrubs, which made the hole inaccessible from the far side of the stream, but it was an ideal spot to find the sort of large brown trout we were after. The river was clear and about fifty feet wide, while a swift current flowed through the center, which was about five feet deep. I waded out in the stream up to my hips in the swift current. I secured my footing and began attempting the somewhat long cast below the brush on the far side of the stream. Between the fast current and overhanging branches I was really struggling to get a decent drift with my fly.

That's when I noticed my last friend who had made the hike with me. He had walked upstream forty yards so he wouldn't disturb the hole, and had started to make his way across the swift current. As the water got deeper and swifter he struggled with his footing. I kept expecting him to turn back, but he kept stumbling on. When he hit the center channel of the river he stepped off an edge and his feet no longer touched the bottom for a few seconds. Water was rushing in over the top of his waders and he bobbed along in the current for a few moments before hitting the slower, slightly shallower reprieve of the opposite bank. He was now touching the bottom of the stream, but water was still flowing over the top of his chest waders. He finally found a rock he could stand on so he could get a higher footing. I could tell he was hardly bothered by the water in his waders, because he hadn't stopped smiling since he plunged into the stream.

Slowly, he dropped his fly in front of him and let it drift directly under the low hanging brush and into that once inaccessible spot that was now directly below him. Just as it got over the deepest part of the cut bank the water seemed to explode. At almost six pounds, he pulled out one of the largest trout I had ever seen taken out of that river. And he wasn't done getting wet, because he had to go almost a hundred yards downstream to land the fish. When we returned to the car just after dark we found that not much had changed. Our one friend was still sitting on a log at the top of the bank leading into the stream. His waders were still completely dry, although he was anxious to tell us about some of the fish he had seen from his lofty perch. Our second friend was still fishing about 10 feet upstream from where we had left him. When he saw us he waded over to the bank and climbed up to tell us how poor the fishing had been. He had only caught a couple of small ones.

As I reflected on that experience, I couldn't help but see it as a life lesson. Although each of us had visions of catching huge trout on our little excursion, we had all used different approaches, each of which involved different levels of engagement:

Talk About It

The first and lowest level of engagement with regard to a vision is to talk about it. Unfortunately, most of us engage at this level in most aspects of our lives. We talk about making more money, finding that special relationship, losing weight, eating better, or catching trout. When we engage in something at the level of just talking about it nothing really happens. Sometimes, talking about something we want or about a dream we have is helpful in creating a solid foundation for a vision. But it's not a vision when we stay in the "talking about it" mode, because we haven't yet taken any of the risks, in terms of time, effort, or money, that are essential for a vision to truly take shape. They are like my friend who stayed on shore and talked about where the fish were likely to be instead of engaging in fishing.

Do what's convenient

The second level of engagement is to do only what's convenient. My friend who never ventured more than 50 yards from the car engaged at this level. Because so many people engage at the "what's convenient" level in life, we are less likely to find any rewards or make any impact when we play there.

One friend of mine is a big advocate of the environment. She reads books, buys organic products and does more than talk a lot about how we need to clean up the planet. Her father lives in Washington State, where they have three different garbage cans for different types of recycling. Every time she visits her father, my friend comments on how important it is to recycle and how she wishes we had recycling in our community.

The truth is that we do have recycling in our community; it's just not very convenient the way it is in certain other areas. And although my friend was doing more than just talking about the environment, she had only been taking advantage of the opportunities to be environmentally conscious that were convenient to her. At this level of engagement, she was hardly likely to fulfill many of her loftier dreams about having a larger impact on the environment. A few months ago, this friend attended a workshop I had facilitated in which I talked about these levels of engagement. She recognized that she had only been taking the convenient steps to fulfill her "green" vision. The next day when her husband came home, their pantry had been overtaken with three large green buckets that his wife had purchased. One of them was labeled paper, another one plastic, and another one aluminum. Each week she now loads the three green buckets into her car and drives them to the local recycling location.

Those of us who stall at the "convenient" level of engagement are usually waiting for others to engage before we can take action. We are often waiting to have the ball handed to us from someone else before we are willing to play in the game. We're waiting for our circumstances to change. We say things like, "If I had the money" ... "If my spouse would do this, then" ... "When I have more time I'm going to" ... Those of us who engage at this level are willing to risk only what we don't mind losing. But as long as we choose to take the convenient approach, our results will likely never change.

Do what's Safe

My own cautious approach to fishing during that trip with my friends is a good illustration of this third approach to Vision. I went beyond what was convenient and put a lot of effort into hiking far from the car. But I stopped when I started to get uncomfortable. I was willing to go as far as I could while still feeling safe. When the water started pushing harder against my legs and I worried about falling, I decided that I had gone far enough. The funny part for me, in retrospect, was one of my primary reasons for playing it safe: I didn't want water in my waders. I didn't want to be uncomfortable, even though the circumstances didn't really present significant, life-threatening safety issues. Many of us are similarly hesitant to push past our own internal, practiced, comfort-zone boundaries. In other words, we say we want dramatically different results without being willing to apply dramatic changes to our levels of engagement.

Often, our own definitions of "safety" have much more to do with emotional security than they do with physical security. Fear of failure and rejection, or insecurities regarding our abilities to succeed, can be formidable — sometimes overwhelming, — obstacles. We may fear how others see us and worry about imposing on others or making them uncomfortable. Sometimes the safety issue that holds us back is financial. Those of us who engage at the safe level tend to apply financial resources to our vision only to the extent that we don't jeopardize our financial safety net. The same can be said for the time and emotion we are willing to expend. Taking the safe route may get us, at best, an "A for effort"; we will, nonetheless, reap a mere fraction of the rewards that would be available to us for going "all in."

Immersion

The final and highest level of engagement is immersion. This approach was demonstrated, of course, by my fly-fishing friend who was willing to lose his footing a bit and get drenched in order to reel in an enormous fish. It is this willingness to immerse ourselves that gives us the power to fulfill our visions, even though we might feel, at times, like we're in over our heads. Those who have learned to immerse themselves in their visions in order to achieve them have traded in "wish lists" for "to-do lists." They have learned how to focus on the crucial elements of their visions and to attack them with an all-consuming vengeance. And just as immersion offers far better prospects for wild success, it also presents more opportunities for crash-and-burn failure. Those who immerse themselves in their life's visions, in fact, have some of the most spectacular failures I've ever witnessed. That being said, they also consistently experience much higher, almost unimaginable, levels of success. These are the people, in fact, who are guaranteed to succeed over time, just like casinos are guaranteed to win if their patrons gamble long enough.

In the case of my friend, and her passion for the environment, "immersion" might translate into coordinating neighborhood recycling efforts, working with local government and waste disposal companies to make it easier to recycle, creating political lobbies, for-profit businesses, education forums and even national or global movements. Or she could find other established groups that mirror or support her vision and offer to contribute to their efforts. Whatever form her total immersion in her vision might take, she would undoubtedly progress to a satisfying, unprecedented degree, because immersion—be it in business, work, marriage, parenting, politics, or humanitarian causes—brings forth success. For those who immerse themselves in this way, failure is not an option. This level of immersion brings to mind the strategy of Hernando Cortez when he first landed on the Yucatan Peninsula. "Burn the ships," he had told his men. "If we are going home, we are going home in their ships." That's what you call "all in." Just think of anyone you may know who has engulfed themselves in their vision or cause and you will see what I mean.

Average People		Successful People
Dip their toe in the water, talk about it, do what's convenicnt, do what's safe		*Immerse themselves in their vision*

Our visions can't become reality until we are willing to engage in them at this higher level. As we surrender to our vision voluntarily, as opposed to doing so on someone else's terms, a new dimension emerges in our lives. Learning accelerates, failures become opportunities to learn, and rather than clinging to our preconceived notions of who we are, how things work, and how things ought to be, we are open to new ideas and possibilities, moving fluidly toward our vision, allowing it to serve as our guiding beacon that can lead us past the status quo.

I should reiterate that the first three approaches I discussed earlier are nothing to condemn. They are actually essential steps by which we can develop a vision. But until we're ready to jump all the way in, the vision will never progress past the fantasy stage. Until we're willing to do this, we feel stuck instead of moving forward. I went through each of these different approaches in developing this book. Initially the concept for the "5 Laws" came as I started analyzing the gaps between the successes and failures of the people I worked with. For the first six months I talked about it … a lot. Anytime I could grab someone's time for a few minutes I would map out, pontificate, and bend many an ear over the 5 Laws concept. The initial laws even started to change with these discussions; it was a healthy part of the overall process for me even though I was stuck at that stage for far too long.

In time, the laws had become refined enough that I knew it was time to move up to another level. This was because I had discussed it enough times and with enough people to feel comfortable making an investment in the concept beyond just talking about it. I was also starting to feel a sense of stagnation by merely talking about it with people. So I got together with some partners and began branding the concept. Before long, and with relatively little investment, we had a memorable look for the 5 Laws concept. We were fortunate enough to have a brilliant designer already on staff, so our initial investment was minimal and convenient. We only tapped into resources we already had at our disposal. But even at that time, after applying the design to the informational materials I had already prepared, we all realized that what we really needed was a full-fledged book. But I wasn't prepared to make the financial, spiritual, emotional, and time commitment of developing the 5 Laws concept into book format.

For me it was easier to implement the concepts of the 5 Laws in the seminars I was already teaching than it was to begin writing a book. I felt much more proficient and comfortable communicating concepts verbally than putting them in writing. So even though it required significant amounts of time to re-brand some of our materials and to develop an effective workshop on the 5 Laws, I was still within my comfort zone. Compared with leading a workshop, there is a daunting level of permanence one contends with when writing a book, and I was all too aware of this. For months and months my workshop bio would include a sentence that required seemingly constant updating: "Brett's first book will be published this fall ... winter ... spring ... summer ... fall," and so on. I eventually took the sentence out of my bio entirely because I knew deep down that I wasn't really committed to the book-writing process. I was stuck in what, for me, was the safest way of getting these ideas in circulation even though I was only impacting a fraction of the people I had initially envisioned. I hadn't yet been truly willing to get my heart and soul into writing the book, so I wasn't really living the vision to which I'd already paid more than a little bit of lip service. Hundreds of times over the last few years I found myself facing that question of "When is the book coming out?" with a weak answer that pushed the target into the future.

At last, when I couldn't stand the effects of procrastination any longer, I woke up one morning and called up my partners. I told them what I was doing and asked them to be patient with me for a couple of months while I lost myself in getting the book done. They agreed, and I started the grueling process of articulating, in extended form, the 5 Laws concept in writing. I ate, drank, and slept the book for months. I opened myself up for feedback, relishing the criticisms, challenges, and insights of others. I spent thousands of hours in front of a computer screen, passing up numerous opportunities to engage in more pleasurable pursuits, which more than a few people can attest to. I made agreements with family, partners, friends, and even clients that I would be available to spend far more time with them after I finished this project. I also asked them to push me, which they did. Now that the book is finished, I relate this process to you not to lay claim to a Pulitzer Prize, but to demonstrate that when I discuss the difference between feeling stagnation and forward motion, as well as the personal satisfaction that comes with fulfilling a vision, I speak from experience.

CHAPTER THREE

Vision Is The Key That Unlocks Depth

A S WE CLARIFY OUR VISION and immerse ourselves in it, we inevitably find wellsprings of innovation and creativity within us that we often never even knew were there. A lot of this has to do with the human tendency to approach life as something entirely limited by time. We map out our lives and justify our results according to time. Take a look at the pie chart below. The entire pie represents the 24 hours at our disposal on a given day. The segments of the pie represent the various life areas that most of us consider to be important. These segments may vary from person to person, but likely include work, family, recreation, sleep, fitness/health, social activities, and spiritual activities.

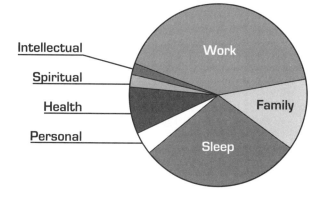

This view of life treats time as a finite resource that strictly governs one's ability to contribute and thrive. Many of us spend good portions of our lives trying to find the perfect balance between these different life segments. The inherent problem with this approach is that in order to increase the size of any slice in the pie, another slice must get smaller. The larger the work slice gets, the more the family, perhaps, represented by its own shrinking slice, would suffer. Or maybe it's health or spirituality that's shrinking. Some of us will even omit entire segments from our lives in order to focus on the ones we feel are important. It's a frustrating trade-off, and most of us are all too familiar with it. But here's news: the perfect balance so many of us long for is an illusion. It doesn't—and can't—exist because of the strictly finite nature of time. And it isn't time that prevents us from achieving our vision and dreams. Just ask those who lead vision-driven lives with the same time restraints as everyone else. We all have the same 24 hours.

Perhaps the worst aspect of viewing life in terms of time limitations is that it hampers our ability to see other options. The continual stress that comes with negotiating this finite resource has incapacitated many a person and can be held responsible for a sizeable measure of exhaustion and depression. In the face of it all, many simply surrender and decide that since there just isn't enough time, there's no use in trying. This sort of thinking—worrying excessively over time segments not in the present—has the power to sabotage all of the activities in which we engage. We find ourselves spending the work day thinking about being at home with the kids, while the time we actually spend with the kids finds us worrying about what's going on at work. At work we dream of play; at play we stress about work. Yet the most successful people we know seem to have an abundance of time in spite of all the same sorts of activities, and even more, that also demand their attention.

As much as technology has made so many aspects of our daily lives easier, it also introduces whole new sets of obstacles that stand in the way of our ability to compartmentalize, focus, and be in the moment in specific areas of our lives. Because of cell phones, voice mail, email, and text messaging, we are becoming increasingly addicted to real-time responses to issues that often distract us from the tasks at hand. When we are spending time with family or engaged in recreational activities, we still find ourselves fielding a seemingly endless barrage of communications that we feel demand our current attention. And at work, we get distracting calls and texts from spouses, children, and friends. While those people who are blessed with the talent for multitasking have a definite advantage in our modern, gadget-driven lifestyle, so too do those who allow themselves to engage deeply in a given activity because they are operating in a different paradigm than just time.

We do ourselves a great disservice by framing our lives as one-dimensional endeavors entirely subject to the limits of time. Because when we do this, we overlook the element of depth. Depth is the secret ingredient known to the über-successful that adds mass to those slices of life that may sometimes appear to us as mere slivers. After adding the element of depth to our pie chart, it would look something like this:

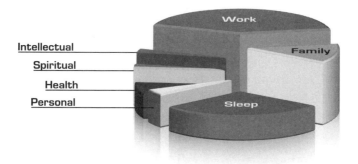

These are the same life segments that were depicted in the first chart, but they are now multi-dimensional, and therefore a truer representation of those segments as experienced by those who engage in them deeply. We all have the ability to change the overall size of every slice by reaching deeper into ourselves and giving more of what he have. When we bring passion and depth to our work, we will flourish in our jobs. When we bring those things to our family, the family reaps the benefits along with us. When we bring them to our health, we will be stronger. Adding depth in this way even makes it possible for one to shrink the fractional value of a given time slice while simultaneously adding greater volume. In a way, we have the power to create time, or to certainly extend it.

That familiar dichotomy of "quality vs. quantity" applies here. Parents can actually spend less time with their children if they work on fostering meaningful, nurturing relationships with them. Managers and employees who bring their passion and commitment to excellence to work with them elevate not only their own performance but also those of the entire team, making everyone's workload lighter. Successful people are able to generate outstanding results using far less time than those who don't recognize the power of adding depth to their seemingly finite resources. And by learning to view their time resources multi-dimensionally, they are rarely derailed by the roadblocks that may prompt others to quit.

Average People	**Successful People**
Focus on life's Balance	*Focus on life's Depth*

For example, one young man I was coaching wanted to figure out how to make more money in his young, stalled out career at a local auto parts store. He struggled with this concept of depth. To assist him, I translated depth into a phrase that I knew would force him into a level of depth he hadn't tapped yet in his work. Anytime anything had to be done, whether or not it was his job, he would reply "I'm all over it." It was a difficult transition for him and definitely ran counter to the culture of the business, where undesirable tasks were shuffled from person to person and left undone much of the time. His newfound commitment to depth in his job meant that he would tackle any and all tasks that needed to be done with an "I'm all over it" attitude. When a new shipment of inventory needed to be stocked you would hear him shout "I'm all over it", getting it unloaded in hours rather than the typical 3 to 5 days. When the door chime rang indicating a customer had entered the store you would hear the soon familiar "I'm all over it" as he dropped whatever else he was doing. Initially his managers laughed at his youthful exuberance. Soon they took notice of the impact his performance had on the store and more importantly the customers he worked with. The customers started asking for him by name. He had started at $7 per hour. Within weeks he was given a raise to $9 and a few weeks later to $12. A promotion to assistant manager and then to commercial manager soon followed with accompanying raises. Within a year he was making more than the manager and other employees who had been there much longer. I'm convinced that if someone was committed to live deep they could start flipping hamburgers at McDonalds and own it within a couple of years.

CHAPTER FOUR

Vision Provides Direction

IT'S IMPOSSIBLE TO IMMERSE YOURSELF in something you don't want. Most months I have an opportunity to conduct a personal development training for four days held at the Great Life Foundation, a non-profit training organization in Salt Lake City, Utah. The trainees are typically 40 to 60 individuals from all over the world. Some of the participants are doctors, lawyers, and business owners. Others are unemployed, or have been sentenced by the legal system. Some are wealthy, and some are destitute. The ages range between 17 and 100. Relatively equal numbers of men and women attend, and all of them hear about the training strictly through word of mouth. Almost every trainee knows someone who has previously attended. The sessions usually begin with me asking attendees why they are there. Most of the time the answers are vague, with "I don't know" being among the most common. "What do you want to experience?" or "How do you want to feel at the completion of this training?" seem like questions that people who have just paid several hundred dollars and committed four days of their life would be ready to answer.

Usually, I have to arrive at their answers through roundabout questions, such as "How are your most important relationships doing?" or "How are you doing in your career?" or "What did the person who told you about this training think you might get from it?" Even in response to such direct questions, most people overstate where they are at in the most important areas of their lives, and more than a few have lost touch altogether with the dreams or visions that initially drove them. By all means, a correlation definitely exists between people's level of success in their relationships, spirituality, and finances, and the overall strength of their vision. That being said, many people struggle to describe what they want out of life even in the vaguest terms. They engage in their most significant relationships and activities with no clear vision of a desired outcome. Without such a vision, they go through life unaware of their potential and end up settling for the mediocrity they've grown accustomed to.

When pressed with these questions I mentioned above, most answer by stating what they don't want. "I don't want to be afraid anymore." "I don't want to be so angry." "I don't want to be sad, depressed, poor, stressed," and so on. Many stall out in their lives because of the low standard that conquering those "don't wants" sets up. "My wife and I have a great marriage because we don't fight." A convicted felon told me he was doing great in life because he wasn't in jail. A drug addict explained life was good because he had been clean for 30 days. Not to diminish the accomplishments of not fighting with a spouse, staying out of jail, or being drug-free, but to express such values in terms of what isn't wanted is hardly conducive to forward movement. While seeing what you don't want could, in some cases, serve as a catalyst for some forward movement, this tactic generally just creates more of what you already have. It would be like calling the travel agent to buy a plane ticket and saying "I don't want to go to Los Angeles." While we may have successfully eliminated one of the cities the airline flies to, it doesn't really get us anywhere.

In my business I face similar responses. My company works with small business owners throughout the world to achieve greater levels of success. When we talk to these business owners the first time we ask a lot of questions about what they want. Most are unclear. Many answer questions in the same way as the individual trainees I talked about. "I don't want to go payroll to payroll." "I don't want to work so many hours." "I don't want my employees to take advantage of me." "I don't want my receivables to be so high." Even the affirmative statements are often so watered down that they have the same effect as the "don't want" statements. "I want to make more money," "I want better employees," and "I want to grow more" are benign statements that narrow focus a bit, but not enough to actually produce a clear sense of direction.

Average People		Successful People
Focus on what they don't want		*Focus on what they want...always*

Far too many of the individuals and businesses that I observe lack the sense of direction that a clear vision provides. Most use the Whack-a-Mole version of life or business in which they stand still and whack problems as they arise. This version of life is based solely on our reactions to what is happening to us. It's a stagnant, unstimulating method that can appear to be much more interesting and challenging than it is, due to the dramatics of the mole whacker. Any mundane problem can seem a good deal more epic when a little bit of drama is added to the proceedings. And problems like this can certainly keep us busy, even though we aren't moving toward a designated outcome.

Worse yet, this approach also misses out on the depth and creativity that comes through immersion in a clear vision. Those who embark on life's activities without any such vision, nor the forward-looking habits it promotes, are like car drivers who use only their rear-view mirrors. Although you can see all the obstacles you've already hit when driving this way, you're neglecting the opportunity to look ahead and to avoid those pitfalls in the first place.

In one of the trainings I was recently conducting, I heard a story that is all too common. I was questioning a woman in her fifties who had been in and out of numerous relationships over the decade and a half since her first divorce. The conversation went something like this (I'll call her Mary):

Me: *"Why are you here, and why did you come to this workshop?"*
Mary: *"I don't know, I guess I want to learn more about me."*

Me: *"What specifically would you like to learn about you?"*

Mary: *"I don't know. I feel like I could always do better."*

Me: *"Could you be any more vague?"*

Mary: *"I don't think so."*

Me: *"What are your relationships like?"*

Mary: *"What do you mean?"*

Me: *"What are your most important relationships like?"*

Mary: *"Do you mean like with men?"*

Me: *"Sure, let's start there."*

Mary: *"I've been with lots of incredible men over the years. I just haven't found the right man."*

Me: *"What would that 'right man' look like?"*

Mary: *"That's a good question."*

Me: *"That's why I asked it."*

Mary: *"I know that I don't want someone who is going to control me, I hate that. I also don't want someone who is abusive. I've done that before also."*

Me: *"That's what you don't want. What is it that you want?"*

Mary: *"I don't want to have to worry about whether or not they will leave me. Actually I've decided I don't want a man in my life right now. I would rather focus on my teenage children."*

Me: *"Is that what you want?"*

Mary: *"I just can't seem to find the right kind of man."*

We went in circles like that for the next half-hour. No wonder she was disappointed with her relationships. Not only was she unsure of what she wanted, but she would also have an impossible time recognizing the right thing if it ever even arrived. This set up a frustrating existence for her that was likely of equal frustration to anyone who might have wanted to be in a relationship with her. Over the next several days as she began to explore what she wanted and what she was committed to, her life outlook and energy changed dramatically.

My conversations with business owners usually don't go much better.

Me: *"What are your revenues year-to-date?"*

Business Owner: *"Through today?"*

Me: *"Yes."*

Business Owner: *"I have no idea."*

Me: *"What would you guess your revenues to be?"*

Business Owner: *"$1.5 million."*

Me: *"Are you on track with the revenue you planned on so far this year?"*

Business Owner: *"What do you mean?"*

Me: *"Do you have a revenue you are targeting for the year?"*

Business Owner: *"Not really, we're just trying to grow from last year."*

Me: *"What were your revenues last year and how much do you want to grow this year?"*

Business Owner: *"I'm not sure."*

Me: *"Do you have an exit strategy for your business?"*

Business Owner: *"What do you mean by that?"*

Me: *"What's your plan or vision for getting out of this business at some point?"*

Business Owner: *"That's what I thought you meant. I'm so busy keeping it running I hadn't even thought of what I want to do with it. I'm not sure anyone would want to buy it."*

Me: *"I'm not surprised."*

And so on and so forth. No wonder such people and their organizations struggle so much! It's impossible to immerse yourself in what you don't want.

Also, focusing on what you don't want in life generally carries with it the negative energy of anger and frustration. Just think about the energy behind the things you don't want. Notice how that energy ties you to your history. Focusing on what you don't want creates those downward spirals we talked about earlier.

"I don't want to be in relationship with a boss who is inconsiderate and controlling." Notice the energy that is attached to that statement. Is it peaceful and forward-moving? Or is it stifling? If you went into work with that focus, to what extent would your boss feel like you needed to be managed, babysat, or controlled? Would your boss be more likely or less likely to be considerate? Would the filters through which you saw things err toward seeing the controlling and inconsiderate side of things, or the friendlier and more trusting aspects? Someone who is constantly on guard for what they don't want will tend to err on the side of seeing, in fact, what they don't want.

Rather than serving as a focus on what it is we don't want, a vision is a fixed point of reference that sets a direction. It is a benchmark against which you can constantly measure your results. Most visions are driven not only by tangible results, but also powerful feelings that would accompany those results. A vision is more than just an imagined desire. It's much deeper than that. Vision could be considered synonymous with the word *commitment*. A vision, again, is something so important that failure isn't an option. A vision is a powerful driving motivator that becomes part of who you are.

Average People		Successful People
See time, money, and other considerations as the cause of not attaining their vision		*Take action despite lack of time, money or other seemingly necessary items*

Without vision, our movement often resembles something we might call the "ant's path." Imagine a colony of ants that randomly wander around scavenging for food. Most ants simply follow the ant in front of them, and if you were to draw a line from the ant colony to the food source they are aiming for, it would most likely meander and zigzag according to chance. Ants stay busy, but they don't necessarily produce optimal results. Often ants won't even stumble across a food source that is nearby because their path of travel is based so much more on chance. And although vision doesn't necessarily guarantee us a straight path, it gives us a significant advantage over the random scurrying of an ant.

The vision-driven people among us understand that one's vision is one's way of life, and not something to be merely dabbled in. And one's vision can encompass a variety of different levels. Most of the really successful people I work with have a life vision. They see their entire lives in terms of an overarching vision that covers every aspect of what they do. One of my most successful clients even decided to replace the CEO title on his business card with the title "Visionary." To him, that description represented the core of his leadership responsibilities for his company. He carries that same visionary mentality into his relationship with his wife and children. It's not surprising that his business has thrived over the last several years, even amid economic downturns, as has his home life.

True visionaries bring their sense of vision into even the smallest and most mundane discussions and decisions. Here are some questions that visionaries might ask routinely:

- "What is the result, feeling, or outcome we are looking for?"

- "How will we know if we've arrived?"

- "How will I, and the others on my team, feel if we are achieving our vision?" (Feelings are an important part of any vision. They are every bit as important as the tangible results.)

- "What will be the indicators that tell us we're on track towards achieving our vision?"

- "Where are we at right now?"

- "What am I actively doing **today** to get to my vision?"

Notice in the preceding questions that results are closely tied to the vision. Knowing what you want and knowing when you have arrived are critical to making your vision a reality.

In addition to applying their vision to long-term goals, visionaries also use it to address day-to-day problems, thereby reinforcing its role in the larger scheme of things. A while ago I was having a particularly sensitive discussion with my teenage son. Instead of the typical knee-jerk discussion that I was prone to have, I spent the time to formulate a vision of the results of this conversation. I wanted above all else to make sure my son knew I loved him when we were done talking. That vision swayed the entire conversation. It was a point of reference I could use to measure each thing I said to him. When I wanted to fall into old habits of frustration and anger, it was the conscious and committed vision of my son knowing that I loved him that caused me to rephrase or eliminate frustrated or angry comments altogether.

Notice the difference between the vision of my son knowing that I loved him versus a prepared script of how the conversation would go. I've at times attempted that mechanical version of controlling an outcome by establishing the script I would like to follow, but I have a hard time getting others to follow the script I've so carefully crafted. Remember that vision doesn't control mechanics, only outcomes. One of my mentors, Joel Martin, taught me the importance of coming from a vision perspective when addressing even daily objectives. She will start each day of the trainings we do together with a clear commitment to an outcome or objective. From what I have experienced, that direction and focus produces consistently deeper results than the normal "do the best I can do" version that I have used in the past.

As we work on projects and interact with others, vision can serve to break old patterns and habits because we'll be better able to recognize that they won't move us any closer toward achieving our objectives. They challenge the status quo when we aren't achieving our objectives. When we're clear on the "whats" (vision), the "hows" (mechanics) will tend to take care of themselves.

Average People		**Successful People**
Focus on how (mechanics)		*Focus on what (vision or result)*

In the 1950's and 1960's, Japan faced a global perception problem. Their products were largely seen as inexpensive and cheaply made, much in the same way so many perceive the familiar and stigmatized label of "made in China" today. One company, Sony, developed a vision of changing that negative worldwide image of Japanese products. This became the company's mission statement and vision, and it consequently propelled every decision they made for the next decade and beyond. Sony started a movement in Japan, later joined by Nissan and Toyota, to set world-class standards with Japanese products. This vision bled into these companies' daily decisions and activities, gradually setting into motion the present-day global perception of Japan as a leading manufacturing innovator with superior quality products.

Once a powerful vision gets the proverbial ball rolling, the other laws can start having a positive effect as well. Lack of motion will foster failure and frustration as well as feelings of being out of control.

CHAPTER FIVE

Vision-driven Communication

OW DO WE APPLY VISION to a stagnant situation in desperate need of motion? I regularly work with individuals, couples, families, partners, teams, and groups to resolve conflict. My first approach is to establish "vision-level agreement." Although I recognize the value of healthy conflict, much conflict tends to arise out of a poor, vague, or nonexistent vision. I often find that in order for teams to collaborate, relationships to heal, and general progress to be made, the effort simply requires a clear vision.

Several months ago I met with two business partners who were really struggling. What made the situation especially difficult was the fact that they were brothers. One of them openly commented on how much he hated the older brother. Any meeting they had would end with one or the other storming out of the meeting. Both had a long list of grievances against the other. They agreed on very little. Each would oppose anything the other one suggested just for the sake, it seemed, of being disagreeable. Their behavior had severely damaged their business and their relationships with other family members who felt like they had to pick sides in the conflict. Both sides were threatening to go into competition with each other and to destroy the business they had built.

In the first meeting I regularly cut off both brothers as they attempted to recount their long history of complaints going back to their early childhood. "What's your endgame?" I asked the two brothers as our meeting commenced. They looked at me like I was speaking a foreign language. Not surprisingly, they had no long-term vision for where they were headed. We began a discussion to outline in really broad terms where they wanted the company to be five years down the road. They found that they actually could agree on most of those issues. As we began to discuss what needed to occur for them to achieve their agreed upon vision, both found it much easier to agree with each other in that context. One of them even commented on how strange it felt to be in agreement over something.

Later we discussed how it would feel to be part of this successful company they were describing. One of the brothers said, "If we were being the company I envision, I would feel respected and valued for what I do and what I'm bringing to the success of the business." The other brother bristled at the jab, but quickly calmed down as I explained we were only talking about the direction they wanted to go, not about where they had been. Both agreed that they wanted recognition and respect as parts of their business vision. Next I asked, "Without locking into specifics, what would have to happen for you to both feel respected and valued?"

Over the next couple of hours they accomplished more than they had in five years as partners. They found that they agreed on most issues. When they didn't agree they could drop back to the vision they had agreed upon and the decisions often became much clearer. They ended the meeting with a vision-based framework and a commitment to create a respectful atmosphere in which team members felt valued. It wasn't easy for the brothers to start implementing the changes, but after six months, they had both made significant improvements in how they felt about and treated each other. Whenever they found themselves starting down the path of disrespect and aggression they would return to their vision as a common starting point. Employees also benefited from those changes, as did the company's increasingly healthy profits.

Vision can also push us beyond our comfort zone and cause us to take actions we normally wouldn't. Here's another example of the power of an all-encompassing vision to set people in motion:

One day I was working in my home office, which is right next to the front door of my home. I lived on the side of a beautiful mountain in Utah surrounded by a number of million-dollar views and homes to match. I could look out of one of my office windows to my front porch. As I was working, I heard the doorbell ring and spun my office chair around to see who was there. I saw a young man standing at my front door. I was engaged in a project and really didn't want to be bothered by a door-to-door salesman. I thought of ducking down behind my desk, but decided that a) it was childish, and more importantly that b) he'd probably seen me through the window from the street. Reluctantly, I stood and walked to the front door, preparing to cut him off from whatever he was selling and to tell him I wasn't interested.

As I opened the door, he was the one who cut me off. "Before you tell me you're not interested, I don't want to sell you anything," he said, catching me off guard. I listened. "I really want to live up here on the mountain someday," he said. "This is uncomfortable for me, but I decided to spend the day up here talking to people who live where I want to be," he continued. "Could I get 15 minutes of your time to ask you some questions?" I could see the flyers in his hand from some of the few homes in our neighborhood that were for sale. I was impressed, but still waiting for the other shoe to drop. We sat on my front porch for the next 30 minutes with him asking great questions. He was simply filling in some of the information gap that separated him from his vision. He asked me what I would recommend that he do to expedite his trip up the mountain. "If you were 18 and wanted to live up here, knowing what you know now, what would be your next step?" My answer was to create maximum value wherever you're at right now. Bring that attitude to your work, your relationships, your hobbies and you can cut your climb up the hill by 90%. When we were finished, I watched as he walked down my driveway and went over to knock on my neighbor's door.

Average People		Successful People
Model after those who don't represent their vision		Model after those who represent their vision

I imagine that it won't take him very long to have the sort of house he wants on the side of the mountain. The young man had a clear vision, and he had gathered far more information than those who contented themselves with merely talking about wanting to live on the mountain. What's more, he'd turned folks like me, who happened to already be there, into his willing allies.

Applying the Law of Vision

Here are questions you can ask yourself to illuminate areas where you might apply the Law of Vision:

What is the difference I want to make in the world? What is my purpose?

What is my vision of closest relationships? What is the vision I have as a spouse, parent, boss, employee, coworker, sibling? Have I verbalized it or written it down? Does it include tangible results as well as feelings? Do I communicate it to those who are impacted by it?

What is my financial, business or career vision? Does it include tangible results and time frames as well as the feelings I want to have toward my finances?

Do I have a vision of spirituality? What would be tangible results that would come from my vision? How would I feel if I was attaining that vision?

Do I have a vision of health? What would be the tangible results of that vision? How would I feel if I were achieving my vision of health?

Do I have a vision of personal impact on others? How do I want others to feel around me? What would I want said at my funeral? How do I want others to feel about themselves as a result of being in a relationship with me?

Challenge: Write a vision statement for your life. How will the world be different because you are here? What impact are you committed to having? What will be the tangible results that others would be able to use to measure your impact (children, causes, writings, lives touched, and so forth)? The final part of this challenge is to share this statement with two people with whom you have close relationships, ones that can start to hold you accountable to moving toward your vision.

THE SECOND LAW
THE LAW OF
FREQUENCY

CHAPTER SIX

The Law of Frequency
(Adapt Quickly)

ONCE WE HAVE A CLEAR VISION, the speed at which we arrive at our vision becomes the next challenge. This speed of learning and course correction is what I call frequency. People and organizations have frequencies. They literally have vibrational frequencies that determine the speed at which they operate. Frequencies are magnetic and tend to attract others with similar frequencies. We can increase these by establishing measurements, measuring more often, and, oddly enough, by embracing failure as part of the process.

Perhaps Darwin's Law of Natural Selection could be used to describe this concept of frequency. He stated that it isn't the strongest or most intelligent of the species that survive, but rather those that adapt the fastest. With people and organizations this law could be stated that it isn't the best people or best products who ultimately succeed, it's those who are quickest to recognize and correct deficiencies.

Years ago I owned a software company that catered to pest control and lawn care companies. Not long after starting the company I had a friend I'll call Tom who approached me about a job. I don't remember much about Tom's background, but I do remember a couple of things:

he had no sales background and no software background. He did, however, possess the most important qualification in my hiring process at the time, which was that he was a friend. So I promptly hired him as a salesman in my software company, since I tended to hire friends and family quite readily.

At the end of the first month I got my sales reports, and wasn't surprised that Tom hadn't sold anything. After all, my training program consisted of putting him in a cubicle with a computer and telling him to play with our software and listen to the sales calls his coworkers made.

After two months, I got my next sales report and Tom still had zero sales. That was unusual in my company, as most of my sales people had several sales each week. However, I dismissed that result, reasoning again that it was just taking Tom a little longer to get up to speed on our software than I had initially anticipated. I also felt guilty about the lack of training and resources that we, as a company, were providing.

At the end of the third month, Tom was still at the bottom of the sales report with no sales. I started to get concerned and decided to pull him aside in the hallway a couple of days later. "I noticed you haven't gotten any sales yet," I questioned him uncomfortably. "What's up?" Tom responded that he had a number of developments in the pipeline and that next month looked really good. Being the great leader and manager that I was, I replied, "Cool," holding up both thumbs to indicate my enthusiasm for his full pipeline.

At the end of four months, I received my sales report and found that Tom still had zero sales. I pulled him aside in the hall a few days later and again questioned him about his lack of sales. He told me about one prospect whose wife had been unexpectedly sent to the hospital for a couple of weeks, which had delayed their purchase. He assured me that that sale was forthcoming in the next week or two. "Cool!" I replied, once again holding up both thumbs.

Five months, no sales. When I received my sales report after the sixth month with still no sales from Tom I finally arrived at the conclusion that I had made a mistake in hiring him for a sales position. And I did exactly what most small business owners do in that situation: Absolutely nothing. I just stopped talking to Tom and avoided him altogether. I didn't want the confrontation. I wrote him his checks each month, telling myself that since it was October, next month was Thanksgiving and then Christmas. I couldn't fire someone, especially a friend, right before the holidays.

Sometime in mid-February, 10 months after I initially hired Tom, I finally got frustrated enough to call him into my office for the inevitable discussion. It turns out that he was actually relieved to reach some sort of resolution about the situation and to find himself a better fit. But my point is that from the time I made a decision (to hire Tom), to the time I was in a position to make a new decision (to let Tom go and hire a new salesperson), 10 months had gone by. This learning speed I have just illustrated represents what I call "Frequency."

Average People		Successful People
Decide after the fact that a result is acceptable		*Decide in advance what constitutes success…and don't settle until they've arrived*

Light waves, sound waves and radio waves all have a frequency. Frequency looks something like this:

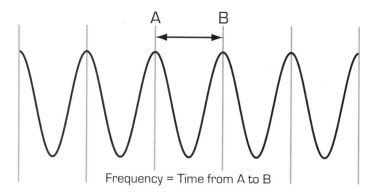

Frequency = Time from A to B

People, businesses, cultures, families, nationalities and communities all have frequencies. In my case with Tom, I had a 10-month frequency. It took me 10 months from the time I made the decision to hire Tom to determine if the decision worked or didn't work and to actually take some sort of decisive action based on the results. Judging from the thousands of business owners and individuals I've worked with over the years, I gather that most, in fact, have an even slower frequency than 10 months.

In my case, I noticed that 10 months was becoming a pretty common timeframe for me to recognize and change something. If I decided to launch a new marketing campaign that wasn't immediately successful, I had a predictable thought process that went something like this:

Month 1—Need more time to get traction.

Month 2—A little concerned, but probably still need more time to build name recognition.

Month 3—At least we're getting a few calls.

Month 4—I don't know what else would work better.

Month 5 through Month 9—This marketing campaign isn't working well, but I don't have time to fix it.

Month 10—Enough. I'm not running these ads anymore; I've got to do something different.

In reality, my frequency was 10 measurement periods. Because I only looked at results monthly it just took me 10 months before I was compelled to make changes. And of course, if I were to shorten the amount of time that went by before I checked my results, my overall frequency would inevitably improve.

Average People		**Successful People**
Make changes tomorrow		*Make changes today*

Another common phenomenon I've noticed is that people often feel like they are making changes even though the underlying concepts and decisions haven't changed and they haven't actually learned anything. If I had let Tom go, and then turned around and hired another friend with no experience, I wouldn't be moving on to another frequency curve. I'd perhaps appear to be decisive, but wouldn't in reality be changing anything. My friend calls this sort of behavior "rearranging the deck chairs on the Titanic."

Frequency doesn't just apply to proactive decisions to do something. It also applies to behaviors, and to decisions not to do something. Perhaps the impact of frequency can best be explained by looking at a longer period of time. If you have a 10-month frequency, over the course of five years you could make six decisions. That's six opportunities to get it right. If decisions regularly worked out exactly the way we thought they would then that would probably be a great number. Unfortunately, that's not the case. Most things don't work out the way we initially envision. In order to impact frequency in a meaningful way, information must be gathered in a quantifiable method. This process of gathering information is called feedback. Many types of feedback, such as financial information, come prepackaged in a quantifiable format. Companies can get profit and loss statements, employees can look at their paychecks, and couples can look at their savings accounts. Those types of measurements become critical in increasing frequency. Other types of more subjective feedback must be translated into this quantifiable type of feedback in order for it to be of use in increasing one's frequency. We'll talk more about how to translate those types of feedback in the Law of Perception section of this book. But for now, let's focus on the essential role of frequency in building success.

CHAPTER SEVEN

The Monkey's Dilemma

I REMEMBER WHEN I STARTED my first business and sought counsel from a respected businessman I knew. He told me the key to being successful in business was being right at least 51% of the time. It seemed logical at the time and simple enough to achieve. I considered myself intelligent and surely capable of at least 50% accuracy in my decision-making. But decision-making became an excruciating process, because I didn't want to get it wrong. I debated for months about taking in new hires. It took me ages to make other major decisions in my business too, such as starting a new marketing campaign, signing a lease, giving bonuses, considering expansions, and even buying a copier. I passed on many opportunities just because I didn't want to mess with my 51% rate of being right. I didn't realize at the time that passing on an opportunity was, in itself, a decision.

Over the last 25 years I have come to the conclusion that no one is right 51% of the time. There are simply too many decisions to be made. And, truth be told, very few of the decisions we make are entirely wrong or entirely right. Most of our decisions, in fact, fall somewhere in between, and lead to semi-acceptable, so-so results. Those also tend to be our hardest ones to correct.

You may have heard folk tales from certain parts of the world regarding clever ways to catch monkeys. One of them tells of drilling a hole in a log or tree and hollowing out the inside of the hole. The monkey catchers then place a monkey's favorite food (peanuts) inside the hollowed out part of the hole so that when a monkey reaches in his hand and grabs the peanuts his fist can't come back out of the hole. Once he has a hold on the peanuts, a monkey won't let go of them, no matter what you put in front of him. The monkey is afraid of starving to death, and if the monkey catchers don't come back, the monkey will starve to death still clutching the peanuts, now rotten and moldy, in its hand. People often behave like these monkeys. They have a hold of something that isn't getting them where they want to go, but are afraid to let go for fear that things might get even worse.

Average People		Successful People
Settle for better than average		*Risk "better than average" for best*

Even when a certain decision we've made isn't getting us exactly what we want, it is often difficult for us to let go, because we may feel like we're closer than we actually are to getting what we want. Sometimes we take the "something is better than nothing" attitude. In a relationship with a spouse we might rate it at a 6 or 7. Most will do little to change a 6 or 7 decision because it's good enough. In Jim Collins's book *Good to Great*, he claims that "good is the enemy of great." This is because people often settle for OK to the extent that they abandon any of their visions of greatness. If good must often be risked to achieve great, then OK must always be jettisoned in order to achieve great. Nonetheless, we still fear that if we let go of a 6, we may end up with a 3.

In some of the training I've done I've illustrated this with a bag of assorted money denominations. I'll ask an attendee to come up and reach their hand into a brown bag that is filled with bills. I'll tell them the bag has lots of one dollar bills, quite a few fives, Some tens, twenties and fifties, and that there is one hundred dollar in the bag. As they reach in and grab a bill I let them look at it and then ask them if they want to grab a different one or keep the one they have in their hand. Obviously, when someone pulls out a one-dollar bill, it's easy to say they want to pick a different one. They have nothing to lose. When they select a five or a ten-dollar bill the decision becomes a little more difficult, but most are willing to risk selecting a new bill. Some stop at that point. When they select a twenty or a fifty-dollar bill then most people stop. They don't want to risk their "good" denomination bill for the opportunity to get the sole $100 bill. The belief that drives this behavior is that there are only a finite number of opportunities. Better safe than sorry. Don't get greedy. But life actually does give us countless opportunities, and when we view it that way, we continue to stick our hand in the bag until we get our vision, as symbolized by that $100 bill.

Let's look again at the concept of frequency. If you have a 10-month frequency, you could attempt six decisions, ideas, or approaches in five years. What if you could increase your frequency to monthly instead of every 10 months? Over that same five-year period you could make 60 decisions. Six or sixty? Which has the better odds of success? From my experience, I would say the person who has a one-month frequency would be 10 times more successful than the person who has a 10-month frequency.

Wouldn't we get different results if we had a frequency like this:

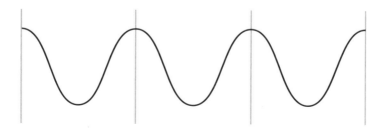

Instead of one like this?

My 22-year-old son Jason recently started his own business, a website for auto parts called pricematchedparts.com. After a few months of struggling, he finally approached me for some advice. I told him this: make a list of 20 things you could do to increase sales... and do them all in the next 30 days. I knew that most of them wouldn't work, but there might have been one or two on his initial list that would have likely increased sales. 30 days later I told him to make a list of another 20 ways to increase sales... and to do them all in the next thirty days. This went on for four months. In four months he had tested and abandoned almost 80 ideas. He only found a few that actually worked. However, his website visits had grown from 11 visits a day to over 150 during that time. He found four or five ideas that were working to increase sales, and his daily revenue was exceeding his monthly revenue when he started the process. From my perspective, I had encouraged him to get five years' worth of mistakes and misfires out of the way in a matter of months. I encouraged him to *fail faster.*

I have another friend who works for one of the nation's leading web analytics companies. He explained to me that his customers have access to instantaneous feedback about their websites. His customers know exactly where their site visitors come from (banner ad, paid search placement, natural search, affiliate marketing, email, etc.) and exactly what they did while they were on the site (which pages they visited, which products or articles they looked at, how long they were on the site, how many times they have been to the site, how much they have spent during all of their visits, etc.). With this kind of immediate feedback, my friend's customers have access to "frequency" at unprecedented levels. They can literally make substantive changes to their business (their websites) on an hourly basis and know immediately if those changes are effective or not.

Professional stock traders recognize that they will be wrong most of the time in the stock market. One professional trader I spoke with told me he aimed toward being right on a stock pick 20% of the time. "How can you make any money for your clients?" I asked. His response made perfect sense. He said that he employed stop losses for all of his poor decisions. If he bought a stock for $30, thinking it would go to $40, he would sell it if it went to $29. That meant he had made a mistake. If he was wrong four times he would lose $4, and if he was right once he would make $10 on that transaction. Indeed, frequency isn't about just cutting losses — it's about doubling down on things that work.

Most "day-traders" who invest in the stock market do the exact opposite. They sell stocks without realizing the big gains and hold onto losers way too long, hoping they will come back. That sort of stock strategy is almost always a recipe for disaster.

Average People		Successful People
Avoid failure by:		*Embrace failure as part*
a) slow decisions; b) no decisions		*of the success process*
c) safe decisions		

I experienced the power of frequency recently when I bought a new hybrid car. Although the car I had been driving was nice, it got less than stellar gas mileage. I was actually excited about driving a car that would get 38 miles per gallon in the city according to the window sticker. After driving it for about 2 weeks I was sorely disappointed one day as I was playing with the onboard computer and found a screen that told me I was averaging 29 miles per gallon over the first two weeks of owning the car. While that was significantly better than the mileage I got from my previous vehicle, it was 25% lower than what I was expecting when I purchased the vehicle. Initially I felt cheated and misled. However, I also found a screen that displayed a minute-by-minute breakdown of my mileage in the form of a bar graph. I started leaving that screen up when I drove. Because I could see on a minute-by-minute basis how my driving patterns impacted my mileage, I would make small adjustments regularly. I still went the speed limit on the freeway and didn't notice any difference in how long it took me to arrive at my destinations. Most of my changes were small. But I was able to improve my mileage by over 33%. I could regularly beat the mileage that I initially expected when I purchased the car.

CHAPTER EIGHT

The Need to Be Right Brings Frequency to a Screeching Halt

Hindsight has taught me me about another curious phenomenon that contributes to slow frequency. Although I had been incredibly slow to make decisions during my 10-month frequency period, I was even slower to reverse or change course once I had started down a path. I seemed to believe that if I never changed a decision, it would never actually qualify as a mistake. If I didn't fire an employee who performed poorly, I could still hold out hope that they would turn it around next month. What's worse, I had experienced a couple of miracle turnarounds — flukes, essentially — that enabled me to justify my lack of action. Inside, however, my gut feeling told me I had made a mistake and that I was simply avoiding dealing with it.

An important factor that contributes to slow frequency is the simple but strong human need to be right, or perhaps even stronger still, the need to not be wrong. The moment we make any type of investment in a given endeavor, we start to lose our sense of objectivity and it becomes difficult to reverse the course we've chosen, even if we know it's leading us astray. Often, being right is more important to people than actually achieving their vision. The more we've invested in a person or idea (using time, money, reputation, friendship, etc.) the more we generally feel the need to be right about it. We'll even ignore results or make up new ones to support our cause.

As I've mentioned earlier, I regularly conduct training sessions for individuals who want to become more successful. Most of these people are leaders in businesses, families, and communities who are struggling in their efforts to progress to a higher level. Part of the training involves illustrating how deep our need is to protect the investments we make. We do this by giving them various experiential processes in which they can participate and demonstrate how they tend to act and react. In one experience we tell the group to act as if they were the United States Congress. They are charged with coming up with a specific action that can bring forth world peace.

Prior to their first session in their mock congress, four different trainers each stand and present four different focal points that could presumably promote world peace. The four primary methodologies for solving world peace in our mock congress include:

Money—We need to have the financial wherewithal to attack world hunger and poverty before peace can realistically be addressed.

Accountability—We must hold people accountable who are disruptive to world peace.

Education—Until we can teach the people of the world and educate them about peaceful ways of coexistence, there can be no hope for lasting peace.

Love—A powerful way to create peace is to simply reach out and love one another. We can do this by example.

At the start of the process the trainees generally have no investment in any particular solution or ideology. They haven't spent any time formulating a plan regarding what they would do if they were in the U.S. Congress and charged with creating world peace. Trainees are asked to select the approach (Money, Accountability, Education, or Love) that they relate to the most and go to that group. Most of the students struggle to select a group, seeing the value in each option. After this selection process, the smaller groups meet to discuss how they can propose a plan of action to Congress. They start to invest in the decision they have made by joining a particular group and focusing on that group's methods and ideologies.

It's almost comical to watch as each group quickly loses track of the overall objective—world peace—and instead gets sidetracked on why their group represents the right way of achieving the objective. Needless to say, when the smaller groups convene as a Congress it's chaotic, heated, and anything but peaceful. Rarely are groups able to agree on any action to take, let alone an effective action. Most of the time, if they do select an action, it's a watered-down, milquetoast approach designed not to offend any of the other groups. It's no wonder that the U.S. Congress can sometimes seem so slow-moving. Watching people with a 10-minute investment in their ideology go to war with each other puts in perspective how some people who have spent their entire lives subscribing to specific political ideologies can seem so invested in being right.

Average People		Successful People
Focus on being right		*Focus on getting it right* *(Willing to be wrong)*

Once people make an investment in any sort of decision, they usually start looking for evidence to support that decision. Consequently, they ignore evidence that might disprove their decision. If you are the one who is responsible for hiring a new employee, you will often overlook or justify any of the employees' poor results in order be right about that decision, even if it means sacrificing your vision. If you get in a fight or argument with your spouse, family member, or coworker, it is unlikely that you or the other person will maintain objectivity or focus on a specific outcome other than being right or not being wrong.

We become equally invested in our behaviors, and often behave in ways that are counter to our objectives. When faced with results that stem from our "pathological" side, we tend to focus on why our behaviors aren't wrong, as opposed to what we want out of the relationship. When I was 22 years old I became engaged to be married. I had a series of tests that I had dreamed up for my fiancée before we reached the altar, one of which was the "camping test." We had a family reunion that spring on the Snake River in Idaho. I invited her to attend with my family for a week of camping and fishing and fishing and fishing. Did I mention I'm a fanatical fisherman?

Each morning before the sun came up I had gathered my gear and headed up or down the river to fish for the day. I usually arrived back at camp sometime after dark. After five days, Susan, my fiancée was furious. She'd had enough, however her being upset had only reinforced my fishing fanaticism. She was relieved to know that we had planned a rafting trip on the fifth day down the Teton River. It was an easy float, with fantastic fishing. Of course I took my fly rod and set out that morning in our raft with Susan and two other people. We floated all day long and I fished all day long, which gave Susan a great opportunity to row the boat most of the day. Some people just don't appreciate good fortune.

As we reached the take out point, there was a road that crossed over the river with only about two feet of space between the bottom of the bridge and the river. Whoever was rowing wasn't going to make it to the side in time and I could see that the boat would be pushed up against the bridge and be stuck in the current. I jumped into action by reeling in my line and handing my rod to Susan who begrudgingly took it. The water was about four feet deep and I could clearly see the bottom, so I decided to jump out of the boat and push us to the bank. (Because there were no rapids on this section of the river, we hadn't strapped down the rowing frame for the boat that morning.)

As I jumped out of the boat and planted my feet on the rocks at the bottom of the river, I grabbed onto the rowing frame to stop the boat. As I did, the rowing frame tipped up at a 45-degree angle for just a moment. Everyone had two hands free and was able to hang on and stay in the boat … except Susan, because she was holding my $%#@ fly rod (as she would later tell the story). She cart wheeled out of the back of the boat, and began tumbling down the river and under the bridge with only her arm, holding my fly rod, sticking up the entire time. I was so pleased to see that my fly rod never touched the water. After securing the boat, I waded downstream under the bridge to help Susan out of the water. Dripping wet, we both walked up to the top of the bridge, and

I could see the blood vessels sticking out of her neck. I knew I was in trouble. She looked at me with her voice shaking and asked in all seriousness, "If I had dropped your fly rod, would you have gone after me or the fly rod?"

I knew the answer she was looking for, and at the same time, I thought of a funny one-liner. My response: "Now Susan, you know my fly rod can't swim…" Apparently, that was the wrong answer. A few seconds later her diamond engagement ring was sailing through the air. I had no idea she could throw that far.

I tell that story because it marked the beginning of a long series of poorly timed one-liners, on my part, in that relationship. I'm still not sure why I did it, but some part of me couldn't resist making a wise crack when things got really tense between us. I had a behavior which consistently interfered with what I wanted in my marriage, which was a close and connected relationship with my wife. I knew each time that I made one of my "funny" remarks I wouldn't like the results even as the words were coming out of my mouth. But I always said them anyway. It took me almost five years into that marriage before I finally realized one day that I didn't have to say it, even if I thought it. My frequency at that point in my life was five years, and it—along with some other equally unproductive behaviors—cost me a marriage before I figured out that there was serious room for improvement.

CHAPTER NINE

7 Steps to Achieve a Faster Frequency in Life

Step 1: Establish Measurements in Advance

ONE OF THE KEYS TO INCREASING FREQUENCY is to establish measurements in advance. Once you have a vision (Law 1) then you can start identifying benchmarks or milestones along the way that will indicate that you are on the path toward fulfilling your vision. For example, if you decided to hire a new employee, determine in advance what expectations and measurements will be used to tell if the employee is on track. Include measurement times. If you want to launch a new marketing program, determine the responses, costs per lead, costs per close, or any other measurement you could use that would accurately measure success or failure.

Measurements should have three aspects:

1. What result would signify success?

2. What result would signify failure?

3. What sort of result would be good enough to indicate a decision or process is worth tweaking?

I envision most human behavior in the shape of a funnel, with actions going into the top of the funnel and results coming out of the bottom. Much of the time those actions can be mapped out to determine the funnel flow. For example, in a business sales process, you might put the following into the top of the funnel: prospecting, marketing, cold-calling, follow-up, pipeline management, referral mining, and training. Perhaps it might look something like this:

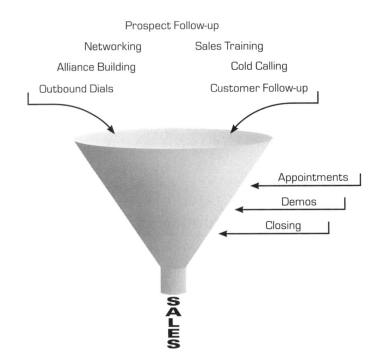

The sales division of my company, Manifest Management, follows this funnel process. We have multiple lead-generation activities that include cold-calling, calling from lists, alliances, networking opportunities, speaking engagements, and existing client referrals. Each of our salespeople are expected to do some predetermined amount of each of these activities daily or weekly. It varies somewhat depending on the sales people. New sales people will focus heavily on cold calls and dialing, where seasoned salespeople will spend more time with clients and referrals. In each case we have a flow that outlines the sales funnel. Each step of the sales process takes them deeper into the sales funnel.

A new sales person is expected to make 40 calls a day to prospective clients. Of those 40 calls he/she should reach approximately six decision makers, which is our second step. Of those decision makers, approximately 50% should agree to see someone to discuss their business. Of those 50% that agree to an appointment, 80% will keep it. Of the people that keep the appointment, 55% will agree to take the next step with us, which is to come to a free workshop to check us out and see what Manifest does. Of the 55% who agree to come to a workshop, 70% will actually come. Of those that actually do attend a workshop, 90% will request a follow-up meeting. Of those that request a follow-up meeting, 65% will become clients. You can see the funnel shape of this process. Mathematically, 100 calls should produce 1.35 sales. My best sales people can produce or beat these results regularly. For my newer or weaker sales people we can tell exactly where the breakdowns are occurring.

While we definitely keep an eye on the final sales numbers, we can often identify problems earlier and specify how they can be resolved by watching the indicating activities. With any sales person I could have issues with the very front-end activity (calls) or with getting through gatekeepers and decision makers, or with building commitments for appointments, or with getting people to commit to or attend a seminar. Each of those steps requires different skill sets and training to overcome problems. As salespeople resolve those issues and follow the process, the most important number to monitor becomes the calls, not the sales. Calls can be predictive of future sales if I work on correcting the course at each step of the way.

Likewise, in relationships there are certain indicating activities that can become predictive of long-term success or failure. People become frustrated because they don't feel safe, don't trust, aren't confident, or don't feel respected or valued. Most people will have a tendency to focus exclusively on the outcomes they want from a relationship, without addressing the indicating activities associated with such an outcome. Someone who wants trust generally won't just decide one day to trust. Rather, it requires honesty as a precursor. Confidence only comes after success—never before. Prior to experiencing success, a person must rely on courage to take a risk into the unknown. Once someone has taken such a risk and experienced success, then confidence can start taking hold. Just as sales won't happen without calls, confidence won't happen without courage.

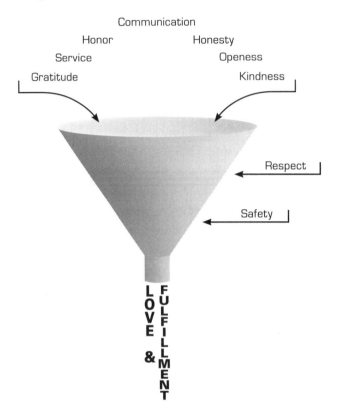

Those who are willing to put the causal action into the top of the funnel and find ways to measure being on track are far more likely to get that which they desire from the bottom of the funnel. As we listen, remain honest, and express gratitude (top of the funnel), we will foster respect and safety, which are precursors to love and fulfillment (bottom of the funnel). In other words, love and fulfillment can be attained by starting with small daily steps that build those desirable feelings and outcomes. Often we don't engage in the behaviors that lead to those because we don't experience the end results, similar to a business that doesn't market because they don't have sales. To effectively change outcomes in relationships, it's critical that we first focus on the initiating activities and behaviors that we each control.

We can start this process anytime by practicing any number of "top of the funnel" activities. If we were to wake up one morning committed to be people who regularly expressed gratitude, we would likely start to gain respect and to connect with those we came in contact with immediately. If the commitment of expressing gratitude became a habit, we'd certainly affect more people. As an increasing number of people felt appreciated, respected and safe around us, we would find ourselves surrounded by much more love and fulfillment. And the more effective activity that goes into that funnel, the more (and faster) good results will come through the other end.

Now that we've established the importance of activity at the top of the funnel, it's important to note that top of the funnel activity can also be ineffective and basically become busy work. Establishing effective ways to measure how we're doing and the results we expect from indicating activities is a critical step in identifying where we need to work or focus. It determines whether we continue with an activity, do more of it, tweak it, or eliminate it altogether. Having measurements in place will cause us to examine our activities and creatively improve or eliminate ones that aren't as effective.

Effective measurement questions might include:

"What is our vision, the result, outcome, or feeling that we are going after?"

"What areas do we want to measure that will indicate if we are on or off track?"

"How often can we measure these areas?"

"What will we do if the measurements do show us to be off track?"

Establishing measurements in advance is a powerful starting point for increasing frequency. When we leave success open to interpretation by a number of people, we will dramatically slow down our frequency. Most importantly, defining results in advance fends off one of our most destructive human tendencies — the need to be right. When we go into a decision open to the fact that we may be wrong, we are also opening ourself to untapped resources of creativity and power. Some will say that being open to being wrong is the equivalent to "playing it safe" or indicative of poor levels of commitment. While that could be true in some cases, I've seen many more people ride out poor decisions and mistakes far too long because of reluctance to admit that they were wrong. Again, our bias toward wanting to be right often makes us skew results or flat-out ignore them in order for us to feel better about our decisions.

Step 2: Eliminate Sacred Cows

A lot of us have had moments in our lives when we stubbornly cling to certain habits, situations, behaviors, people, or objects even when they are unhelpful or even detrimental to a given outcome. These are what I refer to as "sacred cows." Sacred cows comes from cows being seen as sacred in the Hindu religious practice. Sometimes we know what our sacred cows are, while other times they are not so obvious. I worked with a business owner who had hired his brother-in-law as a sales manager. The appointment was causing morale problems, and it needed to be changed if the owner wanted to achieve his vision for his company. He openly acknowledged that his brother-in-law probably wasn't his best hire. But in the same breath he insisted that he wouldn't fire his brother-in-law due to overwhelming family pressure. In his case he would rather lose his business than fire his brother-in-law. The likelihood of that business owner achieving his vision was almost non-existent. In reality he wasn't vision-driven—his vision, in fact, was wishful thinking.

Our sacred cows can come in a variety of other forms. The need to be right can become a sacred cow. In counseling and training, I can usually tell when I've hit upon someone's sacred cow because of the energy they use to protect it. When I push against one in training scenarios, I often get a near-violent response. I was questioning a middle-aged man about his background a few months ago. He was acknowledging that he was a workaholic and he had let his marriage slide. He was also an alcoholic. His oldest son had recently been arrested for drug use and had been sentenced to prison as a repeat offender. One of his daughters doesn't speak to him anymore. I asked the question, "So are you a good father?" He exploded at the insinuation that he was a bad father, even though there was ample evidence to suggest that he was lacking in that area. "How dare you call me a bad father!" he shouted. I had only asked a question, but it had struck a nerve in a place he didn't want to look at. The thought of not being a great father was so painful that he had made up an entire story around all kinds of other factors that contributed to the results in his family. What I knew immediately was that his need to see himself as a great father (sacred cow) was more important to him than actually being a great father.

Average People		Successful People
*Are willing to change **some** things in order to have their vision*		*Are willing to change anything to have their vision*

As I interview business owners I often start with two loaded questions:

First question: "What do you see as the biggest problem that is keeping your company from achieving your vision?" They usually have a well-rehearsed answer ready: "We need better marketing," they may say, or, "We need more capital to buy inventory at better prices." While those statements may truly represent areas that need work, I also know that they are probably not the biggest problems the company faces. My second question is often the most revealing.

Second question: "What are the areas in your business that you excel in and don't need to change?" Usually, their answers are equally well prepared. "Our employees are very productive." "They love working here." Or, "I'm very good at managing and training." Often enough, their answers to the second question reveal the "hands off" areas where their most pressing issues likely are. These are, in fact, the areas they'd rather not look at.

My interview with one business owner some time ago illustrates what I'm talking about. His company had been in business for 15 years making custom doors. During this time, they had grown to about $200K in revenue with five employees. They were losing money and had a tough time keeping their employees busy with work. When I asked the first question about weak areas, the owner described the lack of accountability with his employees. I always chuckle inside when I get that answer because accountability-challenged people are precisely the ones who are likely to blame others for their problems.

His answer to my second question, however, revealed his real issues. When asked about the company's biggest strength he responded that he was a great salesperson. He could sell something to anyone he met. I laughed out loud at that one, because he was actually someone who led a company with no growth, no profits, and inconsistent work. He was horrible at sales, but even so, he kept following the same procedures because it was more important to him to see himself as a great salesman than to actually have great sales in his business.

You'll know sacred cows in your own life because of the emotion that you attach to them. To illustrate the difference between sacred cows and something that you just disagree with, notice how you would respond to some who made the following observation about you. "I think you're an alien from another planet." Would you feel like expending much energy to refute such a blatantly false statement? Would you feel a need to defend your human pedigree? Does it cause an emotional outburst? What then, are statements about you that would cause you to react strongly? These are most likely your sacred cows. What's more, when we're certain that our beliefs, behaviors, ideas or decisions will stand up to examination and scrutiny we don't respond with same intensity as when we know we are on shaky ground.

Step 3: Test Unproven Theories

One of the more common mistakes we make is taking something purely theoretical and treating it as though it were time-tested and proven. We treat our ideas and decisions as if they are right, rather than treating ourselves with the skepticism we've no doubt earned with our past decision-making acumen.

As I mentioned earlier, some time ago I owned a small software company that made software for pest control and lawn care companies. As a computer programmer I was thrilled one day when I found a CD tucked inside a magazine I subscribed to. In the '90s that wasn't as common as it would later be. I immediately took it out of the magazine and started to play with it on my computer. I didn't purchase anything from it, but I thought it was a fantastic idea. Then it hit me that I should do the same thing in the pest control and lawn care industry. If I sent out a demo CD of our software it would produce fantastic results. No one had ever done that before. (I have since learned to be highly skeptical of my ideas that "haven't been done before" — there might be a reason for that.) I immediately convinced myself that it was a great idea and that there was no way it could fail. After all, it had worked on me (if you don't count the fact that I never purchased anything).

I called the publisher of the largest pest control magazine and asked them what it would cost to put a CD in every issue of their magazine. They hadn't done it before so they had to see if they could even do it. They called me back the next day with a price for hand-tipping a CD in each magazine. I called the other three magazines that we used to advertise with a similar question. When all the proposals came back it was determined that it would cost $250,000 to send out CDs in all four of the major lawn care and pest control magazines. I started counting how much money I was going to make, fully assured that it would work. The first magazine even called back somewhat skeptical and asked if I wanted to just pick a state like California and only put CDs in those issues as a test. I was offended that they would call my idea a test because it was so obvious to me that it would work. Besides, one of my competitors might get wind of what we were doing and beat us to the punch elsewhere. No, I wanted this to go out in all four magazines, to everyone in those industries on the planet, all at the same time.

A month later the CD went out, along with an eight-page-spread in each magazine touting our software. It was an ego trip for sure. All the magazines hit the same week, and over 120,000 people got our CD within a few days of each other. It was great! All *three* of my phone lines rang off the hook 24 hours a day. My seven employees took mostly names and numbers. The second week the phones started to slow. By the third week, the phones had pretty much stopped ringing and we were able to start calling people back. We found that we had tons of leads that had now moved on to bigger and better things, many of them not remembering that they had even called us. Many were frustrated by how long it had taken us to call them back. We had also found some compatibility issues between our CDs and various computers and spent much of our time getting our demo CD to work at all (great first impressions). Many calls didn't even get answered, and our mailboxes would fill up in the first hour after we went home each day. When the dust finally settled, we had sold $156K worth of software from our $250K marketing campaign. For those who are poor at math, that's a bad business decision. It was an expensive mistake, and it would have been so easy for me to have tested my theories on a smaller scale beforehand.

Average People		Successful People
Lose big and win big *(break even)*		*Lose small (and often) and win big* *(Fast frequency)*

If you or someone else hasn't done something before, then it's a theory! Science calls it a hypothesis. Recognizing the difference between theory and fact gives us crucial perspective in the decision-making process.

Step 4: Measure Results Frequently and Course Correct as Needed

The regularity by which we "course correct" has a huge impact on our abilities to stay on track and arrive at our desired destinations. Once we have developed a clear vision of where it is we want to end up, we can start programming our directional homing devices. The traveler who wants to go from Los Angeles to New York City doesn't just start driving. The trip would likely be longer than necessary due to unforeseen obstacles. There would also be no guarantee that the traveler would even be able to locate New York. The traveler who starts with the most simple of established benchmarks, on the other hand, such as taking into account the fact that Las Vegas is roughly four hours from LA, is in much better shape. None of us would likely wait until we were two days into our drive before we checked to make sure we were on course.

I once thought about this truism in my little aluminum fishing boat. When I first got this boat, I was so excited. As soon as I hit the water with it I set my sights on the entrance to a narrow canyon on the far side of the lake that I fish in regularly. Not wanting to waste any fishing time, I started rigging up my rods as we headed across the large open expanse of lake. I looked up five minutes later to find myself almost back to the dock. I had made a large sweeping circle in my boat due to the fact that I wasn't course correcting nearly fast enough. In this case I needed to course correct much more frequently if I was to arrive at my designated spot at the other side of the lake in a reasonable amount of time. I had also told myself that time spent course correcting or steering could be set aside somewhat for the time spent doing (tying on lures). My lack of time spent steering would easily outweigh any time I saved by being busy while crossing the lake. Once I started course correcting more frequently with minor adjustments, my travel time shrunk and the pathway to my destination became clearer.

Activity alone doesn't always translate into outcomes or results. I know people who maintain absolutely hectic schedules that seem to demand heroic efforts to complete. Some people intuitively recognize that they won't get the outcomes they want from life by sitting on the sidelines, so they keep themselves constantly busy. But if they don't attach any of their efforts to a course, vision, or outcome, they drastically limit their effectiveness. What's more, the busy activities can quickly become an end in themselves when left unchecked or unmeasured. I see this regularly with the businesses I work with. They keep their employees really busy with unprofitable work, and wonder why they can't grow or get ahead. Just a little bit of measurement could help them understand where to cut back, fire clients, or make changes.

Average People		Successful People
Use infrequent subjective (like, dislike) measurements		*Use frequent objective ($8,100) measurements*

One client of mine owned a small construction company that primarily did framing. In our initial meeting he described how well his company was doing based primarily on how busy they were. They had lost money the previous year and were struggling in the current year. However, they had so much work that most of the crews had to work overtime. As we took a step back from the day-to-day whirlwind and started to lay out in detail the vision of where he wanted to go as a business, we made some revealing discoveries. Under the spotlight of his vision, we saw that much of his day-to-day activity wasn't moving him any closer to reaching his goals. It was, in fact, causing his company to get stuck, or at times, even move backwards.

For example, he found that one general contractor in particular was costing him about $2,000 for each house he framed once all of his clients costs were accounted for. Even though the work kept him busy, it wasn't moving him toward his objective. Worse yet, he was passing up work that would be more profitable and forward moving because all of his labor and resources were tied up working on and funding the jobs that were losers. As counterintuitive as it was, in this case he was able to cut his output by 20% and establish a much stronger foundation to build his business. Three years later he has a thriving company that is 10 times larger and making over $1 million annually in profit because he exchanged "busy" for "effective and productive".

When I counsel owners of small businesses, I often suggest employee reviews as important opportunities to course correct. The most common time periods for employee reviews in most small businesses are in the following order:

1. Never;

2. whenever an employee asks for a raise; and

3. annually

And these annual reviews are a distant third. I suggest quarterly reviews when an employee is on track and hitting benchmarks, and much more frequent (even daily) when an employee is off course. Remember Newton's Law from Section 1? Objects in motion tend to stay in motion at the same speed and direction. Without constant correction, poor results will be perpetuated.

If you get off track enough times, you will tend to lose sight of your vision altogether. Frequent course correction accomplishes two tasks:

1. It forces you to constantly align with your vision; and

2. it allows you to make smaller adjustments that will prevent needing to perform a complete strategic overhaul.

Step 5: Reward Creativity and Contributions

High frequency is often a group dynamic. That being the case, the way we interact with others determines the frequency of the group. Few people give others the leeway to make mistakes that they tend to give themselves.

I once watched a study on TV that explored different methods of training pigeons. The objective of the experiment was to get a pigeon to walk through an entrance in one side of a box, cross the box, and push a lever on the other side of the box. When it pushed the lever, then a food pellet would drop, rewarding the pigeon. The first problem was getting the pigeon to the place in the box that was close to the lever.

One of the attempted solutions involved putting electrodes around the inside of the box where the pigeon wasn't supposed to be. The thinking here was that if it was painful enough for the bird to be in the wrong place, it would soon learn to go to the right part of the box and push the lever. What happened instead was that the pigeons would run to the center of the box and stand there without moving. For the pigeons, the pain of making a mistake wasn't worth the possibility of being rewarded.

People often behave the same way. It can become so painful for us to make a mistake that the safest answer or solution to a problem is to not do anything, or to hide mistakes and stop making decisions. This sort of behavior makes for slow frequencies. With people and pigeons alike, rewards for attempts to solve problems, even if the attempts don't work, make for stronger results in the long run. Successful people are masters at rewarding those who even attempt to solve a problem, because those who are always looking for ways to solve problems—rather than allowing problems to become roadblocks—are those who will inevitably contribute to forward movement over and over again.

One business owner I worked with owned a large construction company. He had been struggling with one of his foremen, who he felt was unwilling to make any decisions. One day I watched as the foreman came into the owner's office and handed a receipt to the company bookkeeper for a saw blade he had just purchased that day from Home Depot. It seems that one of the crews had a saw blade break at a job site that happened to be close to that store. He made a decision to run over and purchase a new one for $79. The foreman recognized that the crew was at a standstill without the blade and figured his first priority was to get them back to work as quickly as possible. He bought the blade with his personal credit card, thinking he would be reimbursed.

Just as he was turning in the receipt, the owner of the company walked by and questioned what was happening. When told of the expense, the owner responded with exasperation, "Don't you know that we have a whole drawer full of saw blades? We buy them in 10-packs to save money. Why didn't you call me and ask me if we had any at the office?" The employee was embarrassed, frustrated and angry. I'm sure he was vowing to never again take a risk in order to solve a problem for the company. It this case, the employee had even solved the problem in an efficient way, but the owner was too blinded by his need to be right to even see it.

Even if the owner had a valid point, he could have handled it differently. Perhaps he could have said, "Great job getting the guys back to work. I appreciate your taking the initiative. And by the way, we have a drawer full of saw blades in the office. Maybe we should put together a kit of items like that for the foremen to keep in their trucks in the future." Such a dialogue might have at once bolstered the confidence of the foreman in attempting to solve problems, and also address the owners cost concerns.

Step 6: Harness the IQ and Power of Others

From my experience, few in life ever really learn to harness the IQ of those around them. Those who do are vastly more successful than those who don't. Most of us are over-reliant on our own skill, intelligence, and capabilities and go through life placing high value on our own insights, while diminishing those of others. Each of us is smart in our own way, and each of us is surrounded by people that can contribute to our own intelligence.

Those who rely only on their own intelligence and abilities have a significant disadvantage. There is simply so much information all around us for us to tap into or take full advantage of. Those around us will often have insights that can be accounted for on the front end of a decision rather than the back end.

Sometimes the best approaches to this are counterintuitive. One friend of mine founded a successful nutritional supplement company. He was very successful in his own right having built billion dollar brands and owning household-name companies like Fruit of the Loom and BVD. I've watched him closely as he's interacted with others who work with him, and I've been especially impressed by how he gathers insights from those around him. When looking for a new marketing design he has a decent eye to begin with. He also has a team of people that work with him who are among the best and brightest in his industry. But he does something else that is over and above what the average business owner does. He will stop complete strangers, such as servers in restaurants, bank tellers, and store cashiers, just to get their feedback on an idea before he makes a decision. He's not necessarily looking for consensus or even agreement, but rather gathering information so that when he makes a decision he's more likely to get it right early on. He also achieves two other important decision making objectives:

1. He becomes less personally attached to being right; and

2. others also become invested in his vision as they contribute to his decisions and work process.

Step 7: Fail Faster

When failure is embraced as an integral part of success, it becomes much less daunting. Those who can quickly laugh at and learn from failures are far more successful than those who struggle with them. I recognize that this is easier said than done. After all, we define ourselves by our successes and failures. At the same time, those who accept failure, learn from it, and rule out strategies that have led to failure, also transcend it and are much more likely to succeed. Success is as much process of elimination as it is a process of "getting it right."

Thomas Edison claimed that he made over ten thousand attempts at the electric light bulb before finally getting a version that worked the way he envisioned. When asked about all of those attempts and whether they were frustrating, he responded that he simply found ten thousand ways that electric light bulbs didn't work. Each time he found a new way that light bulbs didn't work, he was one step closer to finding one that did. Can you imagine how fast Edison's frequency must have been?

Applying the Law of Frequency

Perhaps these questions will illustrate areas where you can better apply the Law of Frequency in any aspect of your life:

Do I have a clear vision or outcome? (Fast frequency doesn't happen without a clear vision)

Do I know the milestones along the way that will indicate I'm on track with my vision?

What indicators or activities could I look at daily to see whether or not I'm likely to hit my targets?

To whom or what will I be accountable? This could be a partner, spouse, coach, business plan, coworkers, or any other group, person, written plan, or target.

If I'm off track, how will I handle it?

What is my frequency, and how can I increase it?

What things am I most likely to procrastinate doing? Do I shy away interpersonal issues, confrontation, analytical issues, financial issues, feelings, emotion, or other categories of problems?

Challenge: Select one area of life—one issue that you've been putting off dealing with—and resolve it today. Have the critical conversation or take the critical action to move it forward. Make sure you're clear on your vision of the outcome (not how it will happen). This could be a personal behavior you've been resisting changing even though you clearly see it's in the way. It could be a financial decision, an expense reduction, or purchase. When you have taken the action, write down what you learned about yourself and your frequency.

THE THIRD LAW
THE LAW OF
PERCEPTION

CHAPTER TEN

The Law of Perception (Feedback)

"My most unhappy customers are my greatest source of learning" — Bill Gates

OFTEN WE CONFUSE OUR VANTAGE POINT of life as being absolute. In other words we almost always think we see the big picture, more so than those around us. As a result we handicap ourselves and don't gain the advantages that come from different perspectives on a situation. We often discount or ignore completely what others are seeing or experiencing and at the same time elevate our own insights, skills and intelligence. This can be a dangerous behavior and often causes us to take long and painful detours from our visions because we ignore the sometimes subtle and at other times flashing neon signs that others are able to share with us. The Law of Perception has several important components. First and foremost is developing a passion and love for feedback. It can be our biggest ally in our quest for success. Once we decide that we love feedback, no matter what, then the next step of not distorting the feedback enters the picture.

Years ago I had the opportunity to attend a Special Olympics event in which my son, who has Down syndrome, was competing. One of the other participants was also a friend of mine, a tall, 16-year-old young man named David, and he was running the 50-yard dash. His mental handicap in life hadn't diminished his optimism or outlook. The race was run in heats and David was in the fourth heat. Since David wasn't especially motivated about winning, I stood with him near the starting line, attempting to get him excited and ready to "go for it" as his race approached. As his heat came up to the starting line, I asked, "So are you going to win this race David?" He was in the first lane, and he proceeded to look down at the other participants in his heat. He then looked back at me and said with a big grin, "I can beat all these guys, they're all retarded."

I don't remember if he won this particular race. What I do remember is his comment, and how so many of us can live our entire lives with that exact point of view. Whenever I find myself looking at those around me and seeing myself as smarter or different, I use his comment as a reminder that I'm in the right heat. Most of us suffer from what psychologists term the "above average" effect. When asked to judge our own capacity, performance or intelligence, we will typically select above average no matter where we actually stand. What makes it worse is that we actually see it that way. Ola Svenson, a Swedish researcher, found that 88% of American college students rated themselves as above average on their driving skills. Another recent study, published in *Social Psychology Quarterly*, shows that most college students considered themselves to be "more popular than average." In one of the largest studies conducted along these lines, the College Board surveyed one million high school seniors. The study found that 70% rated their leadership skills above average while only 2% felt like they were below average. When asked about their ability to get along with others every student rated themselves at least average, with 60% rating themselves in the top 10% among peers. 60% considered themselves above average in athletic ability with only 6% seeing themselves as below average.

Numerous studies of this above-average effect have been conducted among CEOs, stock market analysts, college students, police officers, and state education officials. These studies repeatedly point to participants being out of touch with where they stand among the pack. This is particularly true about subjective results such as spirituality, looks, and decision-making ability. Our need to see ourselves as better, smarter, or stronger than our peers creates an interpersonal dynamic that clouds our ability to improve our own situations. This phenomenon occurs among even the most intelligent among us. A 1977 study of college professors found that 94% of the respondents considered their teaching skills to be above average. We can safely assume, then, that around half of these respondents were overestimating their skills. Although I don't believe this tendency to see ourselves as above average is necessarily unhealthy, I do believe that the way it causes us to treat or see others most certainly is unhealthy.

Average People		Successful People
See themselves as above average		*See others as above average*

While many of us are more than willing to overestimate our own abilities in comparison to those around us, we are also liable to bend our own realities so that they can match our chosen worldviews, whatever they may be. Optimists bend reality to fit their version of life, as do pessimists and realists. The problem that comes with bending reality this way is that we miss out on opportunities to learn and improve on our results. While each of us will always bend reality to some degree, the most successful people I know have managed to straighten that bend. Consequently, they have a more pragmatic approach to life. They are in touch with the Law of Perception.

The Law of Perception simply means that we are willing to make adjustments in our perceptions and behaviors based on feedback from those with different perceptions. Most of us rarely take time to see how other people perceive things. After all, finding out how different our thoughts and feelings are from others can be an uncomfortable experience. Often, when we do find out what others think or feel, our initial response is to discount it or find reasons why it isn't as accurate as our own view. While I'm not proposing that we strive to weigh any one person's perceptions as better than our own, I am suggesting that those who constantly seek the insights of others are likely to make adjustments to their ideas, decisions, and behaviors that will produce consistently better results.

Feedback

Since feedback is simply information, it is really up to us to decide if we see it as positive, negative, or neutral. When we decide that feedback is negative or in some cases even positive, it is likely to elicit three types of responses. In my experience, the first and most common of these is deflection. When we deflect feedback, we look for a way to invalidate or devalue it by belittling those who provide it and compiling reasons why their opinions aren't accurate or don't matter. When we do this, of course, we deprive ourselves of any of the valuable information the feedback offers us. Deflection contributes nothing to our conscious choices and our internal body of knowledge. It does, on the other hand, harden our worldviews to a point of inflexibility—a serious impairment to those who are hoping for success. Those who are able to make effective changes in their behaviors, strategies, and tactics are those who have learned to resist the deflection response.

Many businesses are all too prone to resorting to deflection in response to customer complaints, blaming the customer instead of striving to make changes to their product or service. Even when customers do have a hand in contributing to a given problem, they still present the company an opportunity to change how they educate or set expectations for employees and customers alike, therefore staving off future problems. In relationships, we often discount the feedback from those who are closest to us because of the many judgments we've developed about them. When we continually deflect feedback from close friends and loved ones, they will usually just stop giving us feedback. And when others stop giving us feedback, we run the risk of drawing the erroneous conclusion that we have corrected our deficiencies and have no need to make any changes.

The second most common approach to feedback is to take it in, but then bend it to better suit our needs. Feedback isn't usually one-dimensional. It can have positive and negative elements, and sometimes it can be completely neutral. When we rearrange feedback, twisting it around to match our agendas, we undermine its usefulness. We all have filters through which we are likely to view the world around us. These include optimism, pessimism, skepticism, "victimism," or fatalism. Depending on the "ism" we favor, we will digest the bits of feedback that match, and filter out the rest. In politics, public relations, and marketing, this process of bending information is called "spin." It's a process that elicits huge amounts of distrust from others and also stunts our development and ability to move forward. We tend to readily see where others are bending or spinning information while missing the times when we do the same thing.

one friend and I regularly bend the same exact information into two completely different directions. She worries more than I do, while I'm geared up to view everything (even things worth worrying about) optimistically. Recently she spoke to a group of several thousand people at an event she had organized. After her speech, one of the attendees gave her some feedback that I was able to hear, since I was with her. In the brief exchange, the attendee complimented her for remarks that seemed to resonate clearer than one of the other speaker's. Later that night as she and I were talking, I could tell she felt a considerable amount of stress about how the event was going. It turns out that she had taken the person's comment to mean that the other speakers weren't doing as well as she had hoped. I had taken the feedback to mean that she had done a great job. In fact, the feedback she received didn't really say either of those things, but we both filtered out the parts that didn't match our own preferred interpretations.

The third way of receiving or incorporating feedback is to take it in directly, without altering it. This happens when a person actively seeks out and thrives on feedback. When someone doesn't have a personal investment in being right so much as making sound decisions and developing effective behaviors, they are able to take feedback directly and see it for what it is. Another close friend of mine, who has enjoyed a high level of success in business, has really mastered this form of receiving feedback. We had conducted a training session together, after which we heard that one of the trainees had not had an especially positive experience. Almost instantly, I responded with a negative comment about that person's inability and unwillingness to grasp some of the deeper concepts we had been discussing throughout the session. It was convenient for me to see it that way as it satisfied my ego and protected me from being wrong.

Without even thinking about it, my friend responded in a completely different way, demonstrating how receiving feedback had become a way of being for him. It just so happened that trainee happened to be in the building we were meeting in, and, not one to pass on the opportunity, my friend immediately got up and found him. I followed; interested to see how this would play out. As he approached the trainee I was feeling apprehensive, and I wasn't even sure I wanted to hear more of his feedback. I certainly didn't feel like he was qualified to advise us on how to improve our training. My friend got right to the point. He told him he'd heard that there were parts of the training he didn't like, and that he was curious to get his perspective on those areas. The next half-hour was spent discussing, in a probing, detailed manner, this person's comments. My friend asked numerous questions, and constantly commented on the person's responses with phrases like, "how interesting," "fascinating," "great insight," and "I can see that," which in turn encouraged the person to take his feedback to even deeper and more specific levels. He even took notes to make sure he wouldn't end up bending the information he was hearing.

I had already discounted much of the feedback I had heard. I had great reasons why some of it wasn't valid, much of which had to do with conclusions I had drawn about the attendee and his situation in life. A couple of days later my friend and I talked. He said, "I've really been looking at the feedback we received the other night. There was some great information I heard. Here are some changes we can make that I think will really improve our training." And I had to concede that the changes he was proposing were very good. I learned that when feedback is taken directly, the one who is offering the feedback is more likely to offer even more information, thereby increasing the feedback's usefulness. In this case the feedback had unlocked levels of creativity in my friend that we'd missed out on in our first pass at developing the training modules. Not surprisingly, this friend has a long history of turning adversaries into allies. He's done it over and over again in his business and personal pursuits.

We often discount feedback by saying things like, "I already knew that," or "I've heard that before," or "Let me tell you why I/we do it this way." These statements don't encourage feedback nor do they provide us an opportunity to listen. These ones do:

- Interesting

- Tell me more

- Fascinating

- What am I missing?

- That's a different perspective

- How would you handle the problem?

- What would you do differently if you were in my shoes?

- WOW!

CHAPTER ELEVEN

Refraction

HEN WE DISCOURAGE, discount, or change our feedback, we miss out on opportunities to learn from it. I call this process of bending reality Refraction. Whenever light passes through different types of material, it will *refract*, or change its angle, to some degree. This refraction creates all kinds of optical illusions. It's what happens when you poke a stick in clear water and the stick appears to bend. As soon as any raw information enters our consciousness, it goes from one piece of universal information into our varying degrees of consciousness. Since we tend to refract information and feedback, we do ourselves a tremendous favor by getting other perceptions and/or insights to compensate for our inevitable distortions.

In physics, the angle beyond which light is unable to penetrate is called the "critical angle." If we position ourselves beyond that critical angle, the information or feedback simply reflects or deflects in a way that never makes it to our consciousness. As we become open, seeking more direct information, we get further and further from that critical angle where feedback doesn't get through at all. To illustrate this, here are some diagrams showing the three ways we are likely to receive feedback. Notice that each of these charts shows us different ways we can position ourselves with feedback:

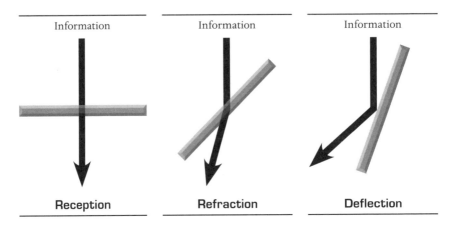

Information	Information	Information
Reception	**Refraction**	**Deflection**

Reception: When we are open or receptive to new information, there is little or no refraction. We position ourselves to receive feedback head on. The information reaches us directly. When we receive feedback this way, the way my friend had done with the unsatisfied trainee, we are more fully illuminated by it. Others will also be much more inclined to give us honest feedback.

Refraction: When we receive feedback with an investment in how the feedback looks, we only actually receive part of that feedback. We position ourselves at a slight angle to receive feedback. The information gets distorted and bent, and although we may benefit from partial illumination, the light is still scattered and difficult to see. When we receive feedback this way, the giver and receiver are both likely to water down the feedback.

Deflection: Deflection occurs when we close ourselves off to feedback. When we do this, we never hear it or see it. We make up the results we want to see and give a clear indication to others that there is no point in them even offering feedback. What's worse, we are less likely to change since we will deflect any useful feedback that may address our behavior. Remember, once light passes the critical angle it no longer penetrates at all—it simply deflects off of the surface.

One co-worker recently experienced the effects of Refraction, as opposed to receiving information directly. At one point, she was really struggling with one of her co-workers. From her perspective, he had been acting as though he were more important than the other members of the executive team even though they all had equal status in the company as vice presidents over their respective areas. What irked my friend the most was this coworker's need to always sit at the head of the table. She saw it as a purely ego-driven move on his part, which was designed to let everyone else know that he was in charge. He did it constantly, whether it was at a lunch meeting or in the boardroom. His insistence on sitting at the head of the table had become an increasingly infuriating issue to her, and she had pegged him as a condescending control freak.

After several months, my friend decided she wanted to redefine or re-invent that relationship. She created a vision of how that would look and feel, and then went to work with a determination to improve that rela-tionship. A management meeting had been scheduled for that morning and the coworker she was struggling with arrived late. Someone else had taken the seat at the head of the conference table much to my friend's relief. When the irksome coworker walked in 15 minutes late, she waited to see how he would respond to not having his traditional seat at the head of the table. He didn't hesitate—he grabbed one of the side chairs and moved it to the head of the table where he asked the person already sitting there to scoot over. Needless to say, my friend was dumbfounded with this blatant power play. She stewed for a few minutes before she remembered the vi-sion or intention she had set that morning of just learning to appreciate this coworker, even his perceived deficiencies.

Average People		Successful People
Deflect and refract information and feedback to feel better about themselves		*Take feedback head on and ask probing questions*

After a while, she felt herself start to soften as she concentrated on the admiration she had for him as well as the gratitude for the gifts this coworker brought to her and the company. As her heart opened up to ap-preciating him the way he was, she noticed something for the first time. She noticed that he cocked his head slightly whenever someone spoke. She had never noticed that before since she had deflected that particular piece of information. Suddenly it dawned on her that her coworker showed all the earmarks of someone who was hard of hearing. No wonder he always sat at the head of the table. He would miss half the conversation if he sat along the sides of the table. By sitting at the head he could cock his head slightly and hear everything that was said. She felt horrible about all the judgments she had made about him.

After the meeting she apologized to him and verified that, indeed, he was almost entirely deaf in one ear. Until she became open to him and stopped bending the evidence to support her agenda, she was closed off from seeing anything that didn't support her version of reality.

Here are some rules of thumb that can help us manage and expand our perceptions so we don't close ourselves off from reality in a similar way:

1. **Understand that perception governs reality.** What others see is the only thing that matters to them. It determines how they act and what they do. Unless we can see what they see, we won't reach them.

2. **Be suspicious of your own perceptions.** I constantly question my own insights. This doesn't mean that I'm slow to make decisions, but rather that I'm open to people questioning my decisions and looking for opportunities to improve on decisions. I actually look forward to being wrong about something or somebody. When I'm wrong, it opens up new opportunities to get things right.

3. **Learn to value the perceptions of others.** As we seek to be influenced (not controlled) by other people's perceptions, we become better listeners and learners and we become less judgmental. We increase our IQ dramatically as we incorporate others' views into our own.

4. **Don't be afraid to learn how others see you.** As we become aware of how others see us, we are much better able to represent ourselves effectively.

5. **Learn to laugh at yourself.** I laugh at myself … a lot. I can therefore attest to the fact that it's one of the very best methods I know for keeping my perceptions in check. I feel that the more we are able to "get over ourselves," the better able we are to treat ourselves (and others) fairly.

CHAPTER TWELVE

Be Willing to be Wrong

Y EARS AGO, WITH MY SOFTWARE COMPANY, I viewed the business environment we competed in through thick, self-constructed, rose-
colored goggles. I thought very highly of my design capabilities,
my programming skills, and myself in general. I saw my competitors
as inferiors, much like my Special Olympics friend, never stopping to
consider that I was in the same league as them. I was surrounded by programmers and employees who were also invested in our company and
its software and viewed them through those same rose-colored goggles.
The only difference between their views and mine was the degree of importance we placed on our own involvement in the company's success. I
saw the company as revolving around me, and others, I came to find out,
felt the same way regarding them. If asked, we all would have said that
we were open to feedback and that we wanted to learn, even though
the way we acted would have indicated otherwise. Perhaps this was no
more apparent than in the manner we received feedback or complaints
about our software.

We were constantly surrounded by feedback—some of it formal,
but most of it in the form of customer service requests. Whenever I or
one of my support people heard from an unhappy customer, we tended
to zero in, on the customer's apparent ineptitude in order to minimize
the impact of the complaint on our delicate programmer egos. This was

easier than addressing customers' perceptions of our product. One time we received a call from a frustrated new client who started the conversation by saying, "Your software sucks." You can image how that went over. My support technician had immediately launched into reasons why our software was the best in the industry. His message, in essence, was "Your perception of our software is wrong." Neither party, in fact, was listening to the other. At that time, I had started working hard at being a better listener, thanks to some feedback I had recently received. I decided to intercept the phone call, and surprised the new client by taking the call myself. I started asking questions, really wanting to see what it was that the client was so bothered about. I wanted to learn.

It turned out that the client hadn't even looked at the software yet, because she was stuck on the software installation, which she found confusing. I had personally written the installation program, so I felt myself starting to get defensive when I heard the client's criticisms. I had designed the installation program in a way that allowed each user to customize the initial setup and to select from a variety of components. But what I considered to be flexible, sophisticated, and customizable, appeared to my client as confusing, complex, and complicated. It was difficult for me not to engage with the client in terms of sparring over whose perception was most accurate.

As I continued asking questions the client finally mentioned her frame of reference, which was a demo CD that one of our competitors had sent her. The client was very intimidated by computers, and this competitor had a one-click install. From my perspective this was simplistic, inflexible, and unsophisticated, and certainly couldn't handle the range of my typical clients' needs. But until that moment, it had never occurred to me that I could certainly provide both options. After listening to the unhappy client, I told her that I would like to start over and that I would modify the install and send her a copy via overnight delivery. It took me less than thirty minutes to modify the CD so it could also include a quick-install option, and the following day, the customer expressed her satisfaction. This became our standard installation, and in later customer surveys we found that it was used by 90% of those that installed our software. This customer's seemingly hostile perception, which I had been tempted to deflect, ended up expanding my own insights. Not surprisingly, most major software packages now have two installs: typical and custom. Apparently my client was onto something.

Several years ago I went through some intense training which was designed to align some of my perceptions of life with those around me. It was really tough. Part of the process involved getting feedback from those who knew me, as well as from some who had barely met me. Receiving feedback from family members and business associates was by far the most difficult part of this experience. When I heard feedback from the virtual strangers along the lines of "You're arrogant," "You think you're smarter than everyone else," "You're unapproachable," and so forth, my first response was defensive. "You don't even know me," I thought. Then I received the same sort of feedback from coworkers and family members. It stung when I first heard it. Some of it hit the mark, and I knew that I could be condescending at times. Other parts really didn't make sense to me. I considered myself to be affable and outgoing, certainly not "unapproachable."

When I quit analyzing it and simply took it for what it was — information — I started to appreciate its value. As I came to understand that others might feel as though I didn't welcome their input and feedback, I also realized that it was their perception, and that whether or not I agreed, their perception mattered. I could either defend my own perception by saying something along the lines of, "How dare you call me unapproachable," thereby reinforcing their view. Or, I could consciously accept the feedback and work on improving those traits that perhaps led people to perceive me as being approachable. For me, this included better delegation, frequent invitations for discussion, offering up my own ideas after others had expressed theirs, saying "thank you," and so forth.

By dealing with these perceptions straight-on, I was able to feel much better about my increasingly productive relationships with my coworkers and associates, and since they had already gotten accustomed to delivering rather pointed feedback about me, I could trust that the positive feedback I was now receiving was genuine. In the end, it didn't really matter whether or not I agreed with them. What mattered were their perceptions, which governed their actions the same way my perceptions governed mine. Because most of us have a vision that involves other people, the extent to which we recognize how our perceptions govern our actions is critical. Unless we are A) aware of other people's perceptions, and B) willing to make adjustments in order to manage, change, or align our perceptions with others, we'll be fighting an uphill battle to achieve that vision.

One of my greatest learning experiences came as I opened myself up to others' perceptions. At the age of 21 I started working as a computer programmer. Not surprisingly, I considered myself well above average in those skills. Around 15 years later I had become the owner of what was probably the largest software provider at the time for the pest control and lawn care industries. My relative success had turned my perceptions of what drove our software industry into concrete. I had one competitor I considered to be my absolute nemesis. The company had a much older software program than us, but we tended to split new sales in the industry down the middle. From my perspective it made no sense to me that they did so well. From a technical perspective, our Windows program was significantly better than their outdated one, which still relied on DOS, Microsoft's original operating system. I was asked numerous times each week about the difference between our software and their software. My response was always the same: "Our software is for Windows, theirs is DOS, and other than that I don't know because I don't look at their software." Not only did I not look at it, I also didn't bother to ask anyone about it. I just assumed our software was superior because I had programmed it.

I spent enormous amounts of money on development. My perception was that the market was driven by technology, and there would come a tipping point when our technology would be so superior to our competitors that the market would have no choice but to purchase our program. Because my background was in programming, my solution to everything was programming. We sent out monthly updates to the software, constantly adding more features and reports. Despite our rapidly growing features list we continued to divide up the software market primarily with that one competitor. My company's structure, incidentally, reflected exactly what I considered to be the market's most important factors—we had seven programmers, three sales people, and two customer support people.

One day I lost a large deal to our competitor. I was so frustrated. I decided that I needed more information, because it didn't make sense to me that we had lost that deal. I knew of six clients from the thousand or so that had our software who had converted over from our software competitor. I would do anything to get one of their clients to come to us—including giving them our software for free, converting their data, and giving them free support. On this particular day I decided to find out why people used our competitor's software. Initially, my information-gathering mission focused on the wrong question, which was, essentially, "Why are we better?" I was so disappointed in the answers from the six clients I called. They refused to say any of the bad things I hoped to hear about our competitor. I wanted dirt. I took notes during my conversations on a yellow legal pad, and upon completing the final client interview, I felt like I'd wasted my time. In retrospect, the interviews weren't very productive because they focused primarily on software features. I wasn't asking broader questions because in my mind I had already decided that the software features determined customer purchase patterns.

As I sat in my office, feeling pretty glum, I started reviewing the notes I'd taken. One comment had been made by three of the six customers. They had commented on how nice it was that we didn't close our support at lunchtime. I had known that our competitor closed its support from 11:30 to 12:30 for lunch and that you would have to leave a message for them if you were to call between those hours. I'd never thought much about that piece of information because it didn't fit within my pet parameters. I wanted our differences to involve some cool software feature that my clients found revolutionary. I didn't get the ammo that I was looking for in the software features, because those simply weren't driving purchase decisions in our market segment at that time.

For the next month I decided to use my newfound insight, even though it ran counter to my entire business approach of technological superiority. Each time I was asked by a potential client about the difference between our competitor and us, I would respond, "Call them today at noon and you'll see." I knew that they would get a recorded message from them about being closed at lunch time, and I was making sure that we, on the other hand, were always well-staffed on our phone calls, especially during the lunch hour. The up-tick we achieved in sales was immediate and dramatic. We would often get a call back from a potential client by 12:15 to place an order for our software. Overnight we began to dominate our competition.

The shift in my company's fortunes had to do with my newfound willingness to take a different view of the market. I realized that my initial perceptions of what drove purchase decisions completely missed the mark. As I started asking more and better questions, and doing regular customer surveys, my errors in judgment became still clearer. One survey was particularly revealing. We found that most of our clients felt like they used only a small fraction of our software capabilities. Our average customers, as a matter of fact, felt like they were using only 2% of our software capacity. I was stunned. Our constant updates and increases in features and reports were having the exact opposite impact that I had imagined. Imagine a customer using only 5 reports from the 400 we had available! That meant that when we sent out a new update touting the 20 new reports we'd added, most of our clients would then be using 5 out of 420 reports. Even though it seems elementary now, I realized for the first time that pest control company owners weren't computer programmers and didn't view software the same way I did.

Over the next several months I made radical changes to our company structure. I started by providing support during regular business hours for all U.S. time zones. A month later I expanded it to include 24-hour support seven days a week. Six months after those initial client surveys I found myself in a significantly different position than I had ever even imagined. We were dominating the industry from a software standpoint. My company structure was now dramatically different with three programmers, seven sales people, and over 35 customer service people. I had learned that customer service, not technology, was driving the market. Our competitor, on the other hand, missed the huge opportunity I'd found by merely bothering to ask what customers valued most from their software provider. They were literally out to lunch.

CHAPTER THIRTEEN

Value Drivers

A USEFUL WAY FOR US TO KEEP our perceptions in check and to tap into the perceptions of others is to understand about "value drivers." These are the factors we consider to be of most significance to us in a given situation. Let me illustrate by outlining my own value drivers when purchasing an automobile.

First of all, the choice I make needs to be compatible with the activities of an outdoor enthusiast like myself. I need it to be able to pull boats and trailers full of my family's various bicycles, four-wheelers, and other recreational outdoor vehicles. Also, because I live in the mountains of Utah, it must be able to handle steep terrain, particularly during the snowy winter months. In addition to these more practical requirements, I have some core beliefs that affect my vehicle selection. As the oldest of eight children brought up in a very conservative and frugal family environment, I have a tendency to shy away from cars I regard to be flashy or eccentric. I can barely imagine spending six figures on a car—it wouldn't sit right with me, even if I had money to burn. So I lean strongly toward affordability when it comes to automobiles. I don't like debt, although I do like leveraging other people's money, so low-interest or no-interest deals really appeal to me. I have strong beliefs about creating win/win business relationships, so I want a fair price but I also want the dealership to make some money.

My car purchasing decisions are also based heavily on the impressions that others would have of me. I recently saw a picture of one manufacturer's newest model on the Internet and thought, "that's a really cool car," until I saw its modest base price. I was immediately concerned about what clients or friends would think of me if I drove a car that was known to be priced at the budget level. At the same time, I'm extremely sensitive about driving a car that might appear pretentious to clients or associates. I tend to focus on safe, middle-of-the-road vehicles that are neither too inexpensive nor too expensive. Therefore, I usually end up purchasing the very high end of whatever vehicle line I purchase. I do this to add a little flair and to make at least some sort of statement about my own image of success—something I promote with my clients and associates—while at the same time coming off as down-to-earth and approachable. This makes for a fairly narrow range of choices.

Some time ago, I read a wonderful book called *The Millionaire Next Door*, which outlines the everyday lifestyle issues of the average American millionaire. At the time I read the book I was subscribing to a point of view, against my more natural inclinations, that "it's important to look wealthy." I was driving a Lexus and also owned an expensive Mercedes. As I read about the more practical side of millionaires, one of the eye-catching statistics for me had to do with the most common vehicle driven by millionaires. It was a Ford F-150 pickup truck. I felt as though I'd been given permission to trade in my Mercedes, which I did, for a vehicle more suited to my lifestyle. I've been driving an F-150 ever since, along with a hybrid due to my increasing urges to "go green."

I also have some other specific personal preferences when purchasing a vehicle. I don't really like browns or earth tones, for example. I also don't like bright colors like red or yellow. I gravitate toward blue, silver, black, white, or even gold. I also like to change colors, so I tend to rotate through different colored vehicles. I typically keep my cars for about four years, and I generally go to the dealership knowing what I do or don't want and get no big thrill out of test-driving. I can't stand waiting, so when I decide to purchase a car, I plan on doing whatever it takes to avoid lengthy paperwork and to drive it off the lot that day.

Looking at the information above, my value drivers, like everyone's, typically fall under 5 broad categories.

1. **Core Values.** These are deep-seated values that typically revolve around perceptions or beliefs regarding right and wrong. They often stem from religious, familial, moral, or ethical decisions that have embedded themselves, over time, into an individual's character and makeup. Often, they are values we not only apply to ourselves, but also that we feel others should adhere to as well. That being said, by seeking to understand the core values of others, we are better able to forge productive relationships with them.

2. **Other People's Perceptions of Us.** Our value systems often revolve around how our choices will affect others, or what we believe it will cause them to feel about us. Although this value driver has somewhat of a negative connotation, it is nevertheless very real. Much of what we do as human beings centers on how it will cause others to perceive us. This goes for the clothes we buy, what we drive, what music we listen to, and so on.

3. **Our Perceptions of Ourselves.** Because we want others to perceive us certain ways, we also make decisions based on who we are and who we want to be. Key to this category of value drivers is our strong desire to feel good about ourselves. For example, when we do acts of kindness or decide to mentor, teach, or serve others in any way, these actions may stem, along with a simple desire to be helpful, from a strong value driver within us to be among those who are "doing the right thing." Or perhaps we feel the need to correct tendencies toward appearing selfish or thoughtless.

4. **Personal Preferences.** These value drivers fall into two categories. The first area is generally directed by our five senses: sight, taste, smell, sound, and touch. Each of us has personal preferences regarding look and feel that are significant drivers in the decisions we make. The second category is more personality-driven, and includes issues such as convenience and preferred selection methods (such as my desire to drive a new car off the lot rather than wait for one on order). Generally there is no right or wrong associated with these value drivers, because they are simply a matter of personal taste.

5. **Resolution of Pain.** These are perhaps the most immediately powerful value drivers and can often override the other ones. Human beings go to great lengths to resolve painful issues, whether they are physical or emotional. Pain, after all, comes from the gaps between how we experience something and what we'd rather be experiencing.

Let's return to the process of purchasing a car and look at some more specific examples of how our value drivers might impact our decisions in life. I'll break down how each of these types of value drivers may manifest themselves in that scenario:

Core Values—Core values about purchasing a car might include the following statements:

- ◆ "I believe we should purchase American-made cars."

- ◆ "I believe we should purchase cars that are environmentally friendly."

- ◆ "It's wrong to spend $150,000 ($100,000, $50,000, etc.) on a car."

Other People's Perceptions of Me—Value drivers in this area might include these statements::

- ◆ "My customers might think I make too much (or not enough) money if I drove this car."

- ◆ "My parents (brothers, sisters, friends) would be so jealous if I drove this car."

- ◆ "The girls (guys) would think I was so cool if I drove this car."

- ◆ "My wife (husband) would shoot me if I bought this car."

- ◆ "This car would really stand out (fit in, not fit in) in this neighborhood."

- ◆ "My friends (dates) would be so impressed with how fast (luxurious, big) this car is."

- ◆ "With this car, everyone will think I'm a good mom (dad)."

- ◆ "I want others to know that I'm environmentally conscious."

My Perception of Me — Value driver statements could include:

- ♦ "I want to feel young (trendy, powerful, etc.) in the car I drive."

- ♦ "I deserve (don't deserve) a successful car."

- ♦ "I'm environmentally conscious and want a car that doesn't damage the environment as much."

- ♦ "I'm practical."

- ♦ "I worry about safety."

Personal Preferences — This list of values could include:

- ♦ "I prefer blue."

- ♦ "I like fast (big, small, sporty, practical, safe)."

- ♦ "I like the smell of leather."

- ♦ "I like being high off the ground (close to the ground)."

- ♦ "I hate paying interest (high prices, full price)."

- ♦ "I don't mind (do mind) waiting for the perfect car."

- ♦ "I prefer used (new)."

Resolution of Pain — These value drivers could include:

- ♦ "I can't get a job (keep a job) if I don't have a car."

- ♦ "My car keeps breaking down and I'm spending a fortune fixing it."

- ♦ "I can't afford gas or insurance on my current car."

CHAPTER FOURTEEN

How Do We Tap into Other People's Value Drivers and Perceptions?

EVERY DECISION WE MAKE is tied into our perceptions of value. We spend our time, money and efforts on people, services, and things we perceive to be valuable. Life is a series of relationships, be they with bosses, employees, coworkers, customers, vendors, spouses, children, friends, or family. Few of us can achieve our visions in life without these relationships, and the only way we can enlist these people in helping us achieve our vision is to find out and provide for them whatever it is they value. Although it's much easier said than done, successful people understand that if they want more from others, they must create more value for them.

The question that often arises here has to do with who determines value. Most of us have a tendency to take what we value in life and impose it on everyone else. The first rule of creating value for others, though, is that the other person always determines the value that you are creating for them. Those gaps that exist between what we value and what others value create a good deal of frustration and wasted energy in our lives, and we make it worse when we erroneously guess, assume, or tell people what they should or could value.

In many of the business trainings that I conduct, I use keypads to poll the audience, a method that enables me to display the results of what they choose on the screen. Often I will have asked demographic-oriented questions at the beginning of the process so that I can slice the overall data by age, income, gender, or any other demographic criteria. The biggest thing I've learned from this process is that there are no absolutes. It always amazes me how differently people feel. Most people severely over-estimate the number of people who likely share their viewpoints.

Also revealing are some of the disparities I see in responses between different demographics. One of the questions I often ask is "What is the most important quality of a great husband?" They can select from 5 options: Good Looks, Honest and Faithful, Companion/Best Friend, Great Provider, Great Lover. Obviously this is not an exhaustive list representing every possible aspect of being a good husband. It is, however, an excellent demonstration about how we often miss the mark with each other with regard to value. The breakdown varies from group to group but typically falls somewhere along these lines:

Good Looks	3%
Honest and Faithful	40%
Companion/Best Friend	30%
Great Provider	25%
Great Lover	2%

The numbers seem to be pretty well divided between the middle 3 choices. That is until you slice the data by gender and see how men rank their own perceived value drivers versus how women actually perceive them. Usually it looks something like this.

	Men	Women
Good Looks	6%	0%
Honest and Faithful	27%	53%
Companion/Best Friend	18%	45%
Great Provider	44%	2%
Great Lover	4%	0%

What's clear from the numbers above is that value, in terms of being a good husband, is rarely dictated by a single element—it's more complex than that. But these statistics also bear out a common husband-and-wife conflict. The fact that such a high percentage of men overrate the value of being a great provider, in comparison with how their wives rate it, suggests that this same percentage of men also have rather skewed perceptions of their marriages.

CHAPTER FIFTEEN

Value Quotient

L ET'S LOOK INTO THIS FURTHER. Let's say that John and Mary are a husband and wife. John is a man who believes that he creates the most value in his marriage through being a great provider. He works long hours, often 50 to 60 hours a week, and makes reasonably good money doing so. He is able to afford a nice house and nice cars, and the kids are able to go to private schools. Based on his version of creating value he would probably give himself an 8 or 9 on a 10-point scale. To contrast this, let's say his spouse falls into the category of respondents who rank "Best Friend" as a good husband's highest quality. How is he likely to rate on her value scale? Let's say 3, or maybe 4.

So what is the actual value John is creating in this relationship? Is it the 8 that he thinks, the 4 that Mary thinks, or perhaps a 6 as you average the two? It's the 4. The other person always determines the value that you create in the relationship. John will nonetheless continue doing what most of us do in relationships, which is work on what he perceives to be his greatest value. He works harder, buys a bigger house, nicer cars, and thinks he's moving up the value scale even though he's dropped from a 4 to a 2 on his wife's value scale. Many of their discussions will reflect this mismatch of values and efforts, with John arguing that Mary doesn't appreciate the hard work and the fruits of his labor, and Mary arguing that he's never home.

In fact, both sides misunderstand the arguments of the other side. Mary, for example, probably interprets John's hard work as evidence that he doesn't want to be around her. In her mind, when someone loves a person they want to be around them as much as possible. John, in turn, interprets Mary's obvious frustration as dissatisfaction with how he provides for the family, because he feels that's the primary way he creates value for her.

Average People		Successful People
Impose what they value on others		*Seek to constantly see what others value*

Here's another illustration of this concept, taken from my former software company. As a computer programmer, software designer, and owner of the company, I had a triple blind spot. I had a huge investment in how good our software was. I couldn't and didn't want to see or know anything else about our program. At one point we had spent three long months developing a huge new release of our software. From my perspective, it was going to revolutionize our industry. The centerpiece of this new software was a scheduling component that was incredibly complex and difficult to program. I equated this complexity with value. Additionally, I had spent significant time and financial resources on this project, so I had gotten so close to it that I couldn't conceive of anyone not seeing its value the same way that I did. I knew that all owners of pest control or lawn care companies would jump out of their seats when they saw the new release of our software.

When the release deadline finally arrived, our entire staff worked until 3:00 a.m., getting out little kinks and bugs and testing the final product. I was excited. I had scheduled a demo with a large company in Oklahoma City, and had a flight from Phoenix that left at 7:00 a.m. that same morning. I didn't sleep at all that night because I was so excited about showing this new software for the first time. Upon arriving in Oklahoma City, I rented a car and drove to the corporate office of the company I was visiting.

The 65-year-old owner of the company greeted me, and he seemed excited to see what I had to offer. I went right for the jugular, pulling up the new scheduling features to lead off the demo. The most complex feature of this was an automated scheduler that enabled users to enter a group of appointments. The scheduler would then process all of them, along with data regarding all of the trucks and technicians at the company's disposal. It would then determine the best possible times and routes and formulate a schedule based on distance and drive time. It was impressive, and could do in seconds, with higher accuracy, what most of these companies would take hours to perform manually.

I watched the prospect's face as I entered the first group of appointments into the scheduler. Within seconds it had calculated the most efficient way to get these appointments handled. The client appeared unimpressed. I thought I even detected a slight scowl. This wasn't going the way I thought it should. "Maybe he's a little slow, with his age and all," I thought. Better show it to him again. I entered another set of appointments into the scheduler. Still no response. As I showed him a third time, he cleared his throat. "I'm sorry you wasted your time flying all the way out here," he said, "but this really isn't what we're looking for." I was devastated. He continued, "I inherited this company from my father and have owned it for 35 years. We've been using the same old mainframe computer for the last 30 years and it crashes at least once a month. Each time it crashes, it takes us three days, with people working overtime, to reformulate and reenter information we've lost. I hate computers. I hate technology. All I want is something that won't crash that can print my invoices. If we weren't so large I wouldn't even use computers." I was sick. Even though my software would easily meet his needs, I knew I had already blown the deal. Fifteen minutes after I arrived, I was on my way back to the airport, empty-handed and exhausted.

In that situation, my method of determining value based itself on how complex and sophisticated the program was. The Oklahoma City prospect, on the other hand, had a completely different way of measuring value that ran contrary to my value system and *the other person always determines the value that we bring to a relationship*. It was a hard lesson that would present itself many times before I would learn it.

When you aren't certain about what it is that another person values, you will, naturally, have a difficult time creating value. This uncertainty, to a large degree, leaves value creation in the hands of luck. Because it can be difficult to measure or determine what someone else values it is often something we simply guess at. When value is subjective it is difficult to deal with or change the value we bring to a relationship. When we find ways to quantify or express value in a measurable form it is easier to deal with. I call this quantifiable value that you create with others your "Value Quotient" or VQ.

VQ can be illustrated with the following chart:

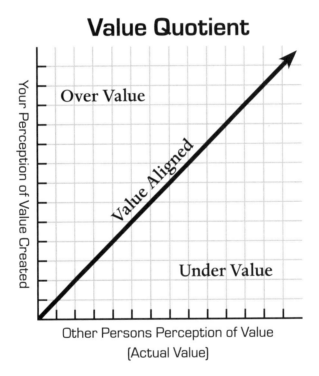

Value Quotient

The value quotient chart allows you to chart your perception of the value you are creating against another person's perception of value. There are three different areas where we might end up:

Overvaluers

We are "overvaluing" when our perception of our own value is higher than what another person perceives it to be. When a husband feels like he's showing up as a nine in his marriage and his wife feels like he's a five, he's overvaluing. Overvaluing makes marriage really difficult, because the way our spouse acts doesn't line up with the value we think we are creating for them. We might expect our spouse to come prancing down the hall to greet us after a long day at work. It doesn't work out like that very often. Employees who make $40K a year and think they should be making $50K are overvaluing. Don't mistake overvaluing with the capacity to create value. They are two separate issues. Overvaluing occurs primarily from differences in where we focus our time and energy. It most often occurs when we make assumptions about what others want or value from us.

Overvaluing is unproductive and usually leads to frustration for both parties. When someone overvalues, they are essentially disconnected from reality. Overvaluing brings along with it several additional challenges. For example, when we feel that we are contributing more than another person recognizes, we tend to lower our performance level to compensate for what we view as over-performing. To justify the current value we place on ourselves, we'll likely refer to past accomplishments that have nothing to do with our current performance. "I was the top salesman at my last company," we may say, even though we haven't produced any meaningful results at our current company. When we overvalue, we are by nature out of touch with what others feel is important in our relationships. We feel frustrated because we work so hard and feel that others don't appreciate it. Generally, when we overvalue, we wait for the day when others will recognize our amazing contributions, while never improving or changing because we see little need. For overvaluers to improve, they require explicitly clear instructions regarding expected results and timeframes. Without clear feedback, overvaluers will inevitably give themselves higher marks than they are actually achieving.

Undervaluers

Undervaluers have the opposite problem. When we undervalue, we greatly diminish the value we create. My wife is more likely to undervalue her contribution than to overvalue it. She is often overly critical of herself, leaving others scratching their heads about her intense reactions. When we undervalue, we are afraid that we are continually falling short and consequently beat ourselves up. Like overvaluers, undervaluers lose touch with reality regarding the value they bring to a relationship. They actually justify their value by making promises related to the future. "I'm going to come in early and I'll work late to make sure things get done," they may say. They usually live in a world of should-haves and could-haves ("I should have gone to college," "If I could have just gotten that other job…"). Those of us who undervalue are often perfectionists who are hesitant to make important decisions and need constant acknowledgment and positive feedback. We take negative feedback very harshly and are constantly waiting for the other shoe to drop. We won't accept honest feedback, instead choosing to read between the lines and pulling out criticisms from even the most innocuous comments.

The Value-Aligned

When we are value-aligned, we know exactly what each party in a relationship values, and we are therefore able to maximize it. This naturally contributes to much healthier relationships. We are in touch with what another person values, and we know exactly how we are contributing based on that value system. Rather than arguing for a different value system, we focus on discovering what works within the other person's system. When we are value-aligned, we do not necessarily expect to score a bull's-eye every time. Rather, we know where we're at and what's needed for us to improve our value. Sometimes we discover that improvement is beyond our capabilities or desires. But when this happens, we are at least able to deal with the relationship accordingly.

Becoming value-aligned requires some sort of method for quantification of value. This can certainly present a challenge in many relationships. Here is a dialogue that might help out:

"I just wanted to do a little check up and make sure I am contributing adequately to this relationship. Based on what you were expecting and needing from me, how am I doing on a scale of 1 to 10, with 10 being perfect?"

Let's pretend they say a 6.

"OK, that's not really where I want our relationship to be. What would it take for me to move this relationship to a higher level?"

Listen to what they say, and don't argue with them.

It might surprise you when you do this that the other person will often respond by asking the same question of you. It's a powerful relationship dialogue. Note that by quantifying the results, we can get a sense of how we can improve the relationship.

As I've worked with small businesses, the most common method I've seen of measuring both customer and employee satisfaction is the "no news is good news" method of measurement. In other words, since no one has complained, they must be happy. Many companies give themselves great customer satisfaction marks because of their lack of complaints. What a terrible measurement. When complaints do come up, it is so easy to justify why they don't really apply. Other common tactics include loading answers for the client and using qualifiers. "You're pretty happy with our company, aren't you?" Yes/no questions like these become difficult to measure. Don't ask for feedback thinking there is a right answer. It is what it is. Use feedback to improve your company or personal performance. Often the feedback from customers, employees, coworkers, and spouses are what unlocks creativity and causes an individual or business to take off.

In general, *I believe that people tend to self-correct when they are aware of deficiencies.*

Years ago I asked my wife one of the most difficult questions I could imagine. "How am I doing in this relationship on a scale of 1 to 10?" I don't know why I was so afraid of asking that question, but I was. I felt like I was a pretty good husband. I knew I had areas I could work on, but I would have given myself an 8 overall. I knew I was in trouble when my wife answered my question with "Honestly?" I knew it wasn't a good idea to ask this question, but I wanted to know how far off I was. I could feel my defense mechanisms starting to get worked up before she even gave me her answer. She thought for a moment and said "6." I wanted to bring up how hard I worked and what a nice house we lived in, but I choked it down. "Wow, 6," I said, "That's not where I want our relationship to be. What would it take to make it higher?" I wasn't even going for the

10 at this point. I just knew I wanted a marriage that rated higher than a 6. I prepared myself for the long list of "to-dos" and personal attributes I needed to work on, already feeling sorry for myself and for the shattered notions of how I'd been doing in the marriage. My wife answered, "Pick up your socks. You could go from a 6 to an 8 if you picked up your socks." I definitely wasn't expecting that, although I could then distinctly remember her nagging me about my socks numerous times over the previous year. I resisted the urge to say, "Socks? You're letting socks get in the way of our great marriage?"

But it turned out it wasn't just socks. We talked for a while and I found out that she wasn't feeling appreciated. The socks were just an example of something I did that sent the message that I didn't appreciate her. Now I saw a light at the end of this "6" tunnel we were in. Even though it didn't create a lot of value for me to have others express appreciation, it meant a lot to my wife. "I can do this," I thought, and for me it was a turning point. I've been much better about doing and saying things to let my wife know how much I appreciate her. Most of what I've done has been small, but I've noticed the improvements in her outlook and moods as I've developed a more acute awareness over what she values.

I've discovered that this "1 to 10" form of feedback, along with providing a useful method for quantification, has another powerful effect. It brings out specific feedback that would otherwise be watered down and generic. It's difficult to work with vague feedback. "The employees feel like you're a bad boss." What can I do with that? When I find out that my employees rate my listening skills at a 6, though, I suddenly have something specific I can work with. At least I can ask the all-important follow-up question, "What can I do to be a better listener?" I can also track whether I'm improving or not.

I've been mentoring another trainer named Spence through one of the non-profit organizations I'm involved in. Over the last six months we have often asked staff for feedback so that Spence could get up to speed faster on his training skills. Nothing improves a trajectory like specific and direct feedback. Unfortunately, most people aren't very good at giving such feedback. Most water it down. Spence would get feedback like, "I thought you did well; still a little rough in spots." It's hard to improve with that sort of feedback. Even when pressed, people would struggle with specifics, mostly because they didn't want to offend Spence.

A couple of months ago we decided to change the way we asked for feedback. We first asked this question to staff: "On a scale of 1 to 10, if Brett were a 10, how would you rate Spence?" The answers changed immediately. We would go around the group and each person would give a 1 to 10 number. The first time we took feedback like this the numbers ranged from 6 to 9. After each person had given a number we went back to the first person and asked the next question. "What was missing from being a 10?" The feedback was direct, specific, and sometimes brutal. Spence loved it and you could see his skill set improve each day of the training. By the last day he consistently got 8s and 9s. He even got a few 10s. What a great way to get people to be specific with feedback. What a great way to measure value.

As we learn to seek out specific, substantive feedback and learn from others what it is they value, we need to do the same for them. It is of utmost importance that we get accustomed to describing clearly and concisely what we value from others. Stop being vague about what you want and let people know! You'll be amazed at how much better they can deliver when they know what you're looking for and what you value.

What do I do with the information that I get from others?

Once you know what other people value and how they see your contribution to the relationship, it actually gets easier. The question becomes, "Am I OK with that result?" If you are, then you can keep on being the way you are. If you are not OK with the result, then the question is "What can I change or do differently so I could get a better result based on what the other person values?" Now it's down to just a choice: "Is it worth it to me and what I value to make the changes necessary to increase the value to the other person?" In other words, was it worth picking up my socks to move my marriage from a 6 to an 8? In my case it was an easy decision involving a relatively easy set of actions. It certainly beat my other perceived solution to improving my contribution, which was working harder to buy nicer cars and a bigger house.

What if I don't agree with how others see things?

Usually, the simple act of not agreeing with someone doesn't cause a big issue. After all, we're used to meeting people who don't agree with us. Because perceptions are just perceptions, they don't require agreement. What does matter is that others feel heard and appreciated. As we ask others for their insights and perceptions we create powerful possibilities for learning and for buy-in. I'll talk more in-depth about the learning opportunities that come from utilizing those around us in Section 5 of this book. For now, let's talk about converting adversaries into allies—even when we ultimately don't see things their way—without needing them to see things our way.

I once attended a conference that brought together peace advocates from around the world. Representatives from various countries, cultures, religions, ethnicities, governments, and advocacy groups were in attendance. Each came to participate and be part of a larger peace movement. Each had dedicated much of his or her life and energy to the global cause in a myriad of occupations, charities and movements. A friend of mine had decided to attend the conference with me. He had strong views of how world peace could be achieved. He was particularly successful financially and saw the inclusion of the business community as a critical component of the peace process. Most of the attendees, however, had backgrounds in academics, social movements, non-profit organizations, religion, and government. Most of them, too, were ready to point the finger at business, greed, and capitalism as contributing factors in the wars that rage throughout the world.

At one point someone made a comment about how businesses, and marketing in particular, were to blame for much of the world's problems. My friend stood up immediately and made an equally strong case for why this discussion or movement couldn't occur without involving the business sector at a significant level. When he was done speaking, a young man from some other country jumped to his feet. He was furious that my friend was defending business and capitalism and couldn't understand how it couldn't be obvious to everyone that what my friend was defending was in fact the problem. It was tense.

When the session ended, my friend jumped to his feet and headed to intercept the young man who had been so critical of him. They pulled together a couple chairs and began a brief but animated discussion. My friend was mostly listening, asking questions about how the young man saw certain things. In the end my friend saw more clearly why the younger man felt so strongly, even though he never converted over to the other's point of view. They simply agreed to disagree.

The next morning we had another open session. My friend had stood to make another point about the importance of extending this dialogue to the business community. As soon as he had finished, the same young man immediately stood. I cringed, thinking we were in for another passionate rebuttal of my friend's remarks. Instead, he was standing to say that it was now clear to him that business must be included in the peace dialogue. Even though my friend had done nothing to convince or argue his point with the young man, the young man had felt heard the previous evening. And in feeling heard, he was able to open up to a different point of view, and even support it, though he still had a fundamentally different opinion. When others feel heard they are much more able to show support even if they don't agree.

Applying the Law of Perception

The following questions might illuminate ways to apply the Law of Perception in your own life.

What does the other person (spouse, customer, coworker, etc.) want from the relationship?

Am I making assumptions or guessing about what someone else wants? I don't assume anything—even basic wants or needs—about others. I've been surprised too many times. For example, I used to assume that every business owner would like to make more profit. Surprisingly for me, there are a significant number of them who don't place that issue anywhere near the top of their priority list. I used to assume that everyone would want to work fewer hours, but there are many who wouldn't know what to do with themselves without their long work hours. Some even love how working those long hours makes them feel. Making assumptions about what others value even when it appears obvious to us is dangerous.

Do I focus on dictating to others or arguing with them over what they should want? When we find ourselves feeling like someone doesn't appreciate us or something we're doing "for them," then there's a good chance we aren't tapping into what they value. When someone isn't responding the way we would anticipate, there is a good chance that we're missing what is important to them.

Do I ask questions before presenting solutions, even when I think I under-stand what we're attempting to solve? Others respond differently when they feel like we have a thorough grasp of the problem from their perspective. Even if we guess correctly about the problem from their perspective, others will resist our solutions or attempts at resolution when they haven't had an opportunity to clearly state what's important to them. They'll actually be looking for areas where we're off track. In addition, the questions will often clarify in their own minds what is important to them.

Am I stereotyping a person or group rather than accounting for individual preferences and biases?

Do I resist the urge to make others feel wrong about what they value? Do I find myself being argumentative when it comes to how others feel, what they like, or what they want?

In what ways do I tend to bend or refract information or feedback? How would others tend to react to or account for my refraction?

Challenge: Get feedback on how you are doing from two people today. Ask this question: "On a scale of 1 to 10, 1 meaning it couldn't possibly be worse and 10 being it couldn't possibly be better, how am I doing in this relationship?" If the answer is below what you would like it to be then say: "That isn't where I want it to be; what can I do to create more value with you?" Then listen, ask probing questions, repeat back what you've heard, and let them know what they can count on from you.

THE FOURTH LAW
THE LAW OF
ACCOUNTABILITY

CHAPTER SIXTEEN

The Law of Accountability (Ownership)

THE LAW OF ACCOUNTABILITY is about the ownership of results. Ownership includes owning our contribution to both positive and negative results. We're all familiar with the urge to overstate our contributions to positive results and understate or distance ourselves from less positive ones. We lose on both counts when we do this, because when we take credit for contributions beyond what we actually did, we will often most certainly impact others negatively and diminish future performance. And when we distance ourselves from our contribution to a result, we miss out on opportunities to see what we might do differently. When we don't see what we can do differently, choosing instead to only see what others could have done differently, then we don't learn anything and are therefore likely to experience the same or similar failures in the future.

Learning to be accountable has three primary benefits:

1. Accountable people engage in a form of speed learning that cannot be accessed by any other method.

2. Accountability brings with it a sense of personal power that is contagious and life transforming.

3. Finally, accountability significantly reduces drag with others. It gives them the freedom to be accountable themselves without fear of reprisal or getting blame offloaded on them.

In March of 2007, Scott Burns, a writer for *MSN Money*, published a column about the poor customer service at Home Depot. Thousands of readers added their posts to Scott's column. One of the posts to his column drew national attention.

I'm Frank Blake, the new CEO for The Home Depot. I've read a number of the postings on the MSN message board (unfortunately, there were a lot of them), and we've dispatched a dedicated task force—working directly with me—that is ready and willing to address each and every issue raised on this board. Please give us the chance.

There's no way I can express how sorry I am for all of the stories you shared. I recognize that many of you were loyal and dedicated shoppers of The Home Depot…and we let you down. That's unacceptable. Customers are our company's lifeblood—and the sole reason we have been able to build such a successful company is because of your support. The only way we're going to continue to be successful is by regaining your trust and confidence…and we will do that.

We've already taken steps to cure many of the ills discussed on this message board:

- We will be and already are increasing our staffing in the stores.

- We're also in the early stages of launching a nationwide program to recruit and hire skilled master trades people to staff our stores so that our customers receive the kind of service and expertise that made The Home Depot great.

- We're investing significantly in the appearance of our stores to make them an easier and more fun place to shop.

- And we're making it clear to all our associates that nothing is more important than you, the customer. Every associate knows that his or her number one job is to make you smile and to help you solve your home improvement problem…no matter how big or how small.

But the real judge of all of these changes we're making is you. All I ask is that you please give us the opportunity to win you back. When you enter our stores, you should receive a personal greeting. After that, you should encounter a helpful associate who will walk you to find the tools, material or service you need. If you don't, please let us know...just like Scott Burns did.

I'd like to thank Scott—his column about our company was insightful and revealing. You can easily tell that it struck a nerve with me. Scott, we'll do all in our power to again make The Home Depot the store you and your wife, Carolyn, once referred to as "our store." I'd also like to give my thanks to the many people who posted comments on this board. We want them. We need them...to enable us to keep getting better. We're committed to being the company that helped set the standard for customer service excellence in home improvement. Please continue to hold us accountable.

You have my personal assurance that every effort will be made to address your concerns.

The Home Depot was built on great customer service, and we hope to rebuild your trust on that same tradition—just give us the chance!

No defense, no justification, no refraction of the feedback. Frank Blake took the feedback head-on and in so doing greatly improved his chances of solving the problem. Notice the positive mood he's able to generate by taking ownership. As you read Mr. Blake's letter, didn't you feel at least some compulsion to give Home Depot another chance?

Contrast this with the way that so many of us are tempted to handle feedback and deal with life's roadblocks. When I counsel with business owners, I notice a significant difference in this regard between those who constantly struggle and those who thrive. Those who thrive are almost always willing to own how they contribute to any of the results that they are achieving, be they good or bad. For example, when I ask struggling business owners about their business results, I am accustomed to hearing the following type of response:

"Well, the economy has been really slow lately."

"My competitors are idiots; they have to be losing money with the prices they are charging."

"Fuel and material prices have killed me."

"The labor market is really tough."

"My employees are total flakes."

Do you recognize these types of comments? Notice how powerless they seem. They focus entirely on external forces, some of which may even be real. But by focusing on those, people completely disempower themselves as they profess their inability to take any sort of responsibility.

Indeed, the problem with these types of statements that blame external forces, even if true, is that they make no consideration for individual choice or power. In the training sessions I conduct, I ask questions about why people don't have what they want in life. Most often, the responses are similar:

"All the good men are married."

"My wife is completely irrational."

"My husband doesn't trust me."

"My employer doesn't recognize my contributions."

I'm doing the best I can."

"I can't trust anyone."

"He/she makes me feel..."

You get the picture. This version of life can be depicted with the following diagram:

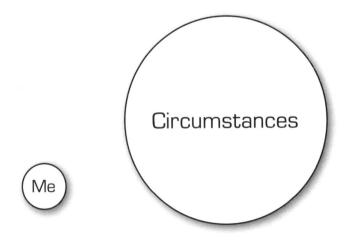

When you see the external circumstances in life as being all powerful and controlling, then this outlook will set you up for failure and low achievement. All manner of circumstances are readily available for us to justify, rationalize, or explain away. The problem with acting this way, again, is that it prevents us from accounting for the choices we made that lent these circumstances such impact. Glaring holes often mar these excuses we make, and they are frequently more convenient than they are true.

I've worked with many construction companies throughout the country during the recent construction boom and the subsequent bust. I watched as various companies responded to the national and local circumstances and adjusted their business practices accordingly, while others threw their hands up in the air. Those in the latter category, seeing themselves as victims in this whole housing meltdown, missed out on a number of great opportunities to learn and to adapt their business to the extent that they could brace for (and thrive in) the future. The most commonly blamed culprit I heard about from these business owners was the national media. "If the national media wasn't publishing all the negative articles about the home market, then we wouldn't be in the mess we're in," they said. Few, it seemed, were willing to take any accountability for the building frenzy and the investor sales that wreaked havoc on the market, along with the shady financing deals that littered those boom years. These were all areas that builders and mortgage companies seemed slow to address and uninterested in learning from. It's much easier to point fingers at other factors than the ones we've contributed to directly.

Average People		Successful People
Look for reasons		*Focus on results*

Recently, during a 10% decline in the local construction market, I was able to observe the disparity between clients who were growing in spite of the decline, and others who had shrunk by as much as 40%. Guess which ones were most likely to fixate on the declining market? The ones who were shrinking, of course, even though a 10% market decline doesn't easily explain a 40% drop in company revenues. Since I'd also worked with many of these companies during the construction boom, I was able to observe a pattern in their approach.

Most of these companies who were struggling during the housing bust didn't fully capitalize during the boom years either. At that time, the labor market was extremely tight. While national unemployment was down to less than 4%, many local markets were experiencing unemployment rates at 2.5% or less. During those times, the companies that were now complaining about the national media ruining the market had failed to capitalize on the previous growth due to the fact that "there were no employees available." Notice how no matter what there is always a reason why they don't succeed.

I would ask these clients if it was the housing slump, or their failure to manage and account for that housing downturn, that was the source of their current problems. Most of them were able to recognize that the second option is more truthful than the first. Recently, when I was working with an individual who claimed to be miserable because her husband didn't trust her, I asked her how she might have contributed to him seeing her as untrustworthy. I know full well when I ask these questions that external forces—like the lady's husband—have possibly had a considerable impact. However, I also know that each of us has far more control over our outcomes than we like to think or see. As she responded to further questions it became clear to both of us how she had contributed to the distrust in her marriage.

When I work with the über-successful, I see them constantly accounting for their circumstances and adjusting behaviors accordingly. Here's how they see their lives (compare it with the previous diagram):

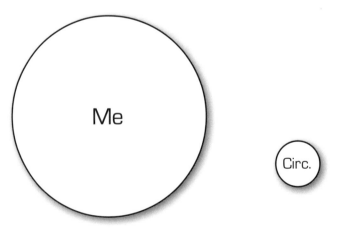

CHAPTER SEVENTEEN

Account for Our
Contributions to an Outcome

A CCOUNTABILITY IS THE PROCESS of accounting for the choices, behaviors, thoughts, and actions that create, contribute to, or allow for certain results to occur. It is of equal importance for us to be able to account for contributions and behaviors that have led to success as well as the ones that have led to failure.

When we deny accountability, we cast ourselves as victims. We can be victims to other people, the economy, our employers, our customers, or any other outside factors or circumstances. Victims are devoid of choice, control, or opportunities to learn in a forward-moving way. From my experience, most people love being victims. It absolves them from responsibility, results, and actions and renders them blameless. In addition, being a victim can elicit sympathy, attention, and pity, which are actually enticing counterfeits for the genuine love most humans crave. They're like saccharine packets—they're not really sugar, but they kind of taste like it.

True accountability, we should also remember, isn't merely blaming ourselves for problems. When we get in the habit of doing this, we become victims of ourselves—our weaknesses, our knowledge deficiencies, or personal quirks. In order to be truly accountable, we often need to go back in time and recall what it is we felt, what we knew, what we were told, the choices that we made, what we ignored, and how we dealt with the events after they occurred.

Consider this builder's accountable version of what happened to his business:

> I've been in business for 15 years, so I've seen housing cycles before. I was greedy in the housing boom and overextended myself on building spec homes. I knew on a gut level that the market couldn't sustain the growth it was going through and I ignored it. I also wondered about some of the investors and even buyers that were buying the homes I built and how they would make payments a couple of years from now. I decided it wasn't my problem. When some markets started to decline nationally, I knew that I should start to pull back, but I ignored it and talked myself into believing that our local market was different. Several industry leaders and economists also told us to start cutting back on spec homes, but I thought I could get in a few more before the decline. When the market started to decline I didn't make expense cuts until long after they would have been appropriate. I haven't adjusted my marketing to account for the changes in new homebuyer patterns. I'm not sure how to sell in this new environment.

Do you notice all the opportunities for learning and changing that find expression in the accountable version? From what I've seen, most of us struggle with accountability. We like to absolve ourselves of contributing to outcomes so that we can feel better about ourselves. In the end, that behavior aids our progress like a ball and chain.

Compare this to one of my own victim stories:

> I live on the side of a Mountain in Bountiful, Utah. One morning I came back from an appointment and parked my new truck in my driveway. I went into the house for a couple of hours and when I went out to leave again I was quite surprised to find a large boulder in my driveway. My head pounded with confusion as I puzzled over why someone would dump a boulder in my driveway. Then I noticed the glass surrounding the boulder. Who would dump a boulder and break glass in my driveway, I thought (I'm a little slow sometimes). Then I looked up at my truck and noticed the crushed cab. Who would drop a boulder on my truck and then push it off onto my driveway, I thought. Then I looked up on the hill above my house and noticed a clear path through the snowy hillside. Two hundred yards up the hill I saw a backhoe working on my neigh-

bors' rock retention wall and suddenly I was able to put the puzzle pieces together. I'm pretty bright when it comes to things that are obvious. Apparently some idiot on the backhoe decided to let a boulder go, thinking it wouldn't roll very far. The rock retention people and the landscapers both pointed fingers at the other group. One even told me that the boulder probably blew off of the hill. What a hassle. The owner, my neighbor, finally had to pay me for the damage to my car because no one else would accept the responsibility. I had to go four weeks without my truck while it underwent major repairs.

Now that's a victim story. A boulder randomly hits my car while I'm parked in my own driveway. We like telling the victim versions of stories. We even learn how to embellish them to make them worse, funnier, sad, or whatever other emotion we want to suck people into.

Let me give you another version of the same story — the accountable version:

> We had bought the lot we built on around five years previously. My first observation when I saw the lot had to do with how difficult it would be to build a house on such a steep hill. I wondered if rock slides or avalanches could be significant, dangerous factors to those who lived there, but I bought the lot and built the house anyway. Over the previous five years I have constantly had to clear my driveway of rocks and small stones that have rolled down the hill. I'm well aware of the effects of gravity on rocks and hills. When I came home that day I parked my car right next to the rock retaining wall that lines the uphill side of my driveway. I was parked so close that you wouldn't be able to get in through the passenger door. As I got out of the car, I had a gut feeling that I shouldn't park there. I parked there anyway, rationalizing that I wouldn't be in the house for very long. My first response when I saw my truck was, "I knew something like this would happen." It turned out to be a perfect opportunity to meet my new neighbor. "Brad, I've got one of your boulders in my driveway." We figured everything out, and luckily I had other cars I could drive. Other than a few lessons, it really didn't have any major negative impact on my life. It's funny how that works.

Of the two stories, the first is more entertaining and certainly absolves me of anything. It may also get me some sympathy and pity from those who hear it. But the second gives me opportunities to learn, trust myself, and to connect with a new neighbor. It allows me to proactively solve potential future problems. And it also removes the drama from the story. Drama is usually a surefire indicator that a victimization story—as opposed to an accountable one—is underway.

As we learn to hold ourselves accountable, we can start building better lives by surrounding ourselves with other accountable people. But this can only begin when we own our contributions and take proactive steps to resolve shortfalls. Accountability has a contagious effect, just as playing the victim does. We attract others into our work environments and relationships that we feel comfortable with—and who mirror—our level of accountability.

Average People		Successful People
Focus on how others need to change		*Focus on what they need to change*

The first three of the Five Laws—Vision, Frequency, and Perception—are critical components of the fourth, Accountability. We must first define our visions, and then lay out the expected results. If the vision and results are not clearly defined, then the likelihood for accountability immediately starts to cloud over. Our vision becomes the basis for what we are accountable for. As we hold ourselves accountable for achieving our vision in different areas of our lives, then we're always off to a healthy start. We should define the results of our vision in clear, quantifiable, measurable terms, so that all parties involved can operate using the same parameters. Whenever confusion exists regarding expectations or results, we run the risk of setting up a structure of poor (if any) accountability. In the event that confusion does arise, we can either do battle over what we or others "should have known or assumed" and what actually happened, or we can clean it up and move forward by redefining expectations and agreements.

Once we set a clear vision in place, we can establish the mile markers that will indicate whether we're on the right track so that we can accelerate our frequency. We must also consider, in advance, how we will handle the eventuality of getting off track. What specific actions will we agree to take, and how often can we measure and course correct? What are the agreements we'll make with each other in clear, quantifiable terms? How can we make sure we aren't bending (refracting) results to feel better about ourselves at the expense of our vision?

Finally, what are the channels we can use to make sure we get clear and specific feedback on how we're doing? How will others perceive whether we are on track toward meeting our objectives? What will we do with the feedback we receive and how will we receive it? How will we make sure that everyone can see the same feedback, and that people won't be looking for feedback that only supports what they want to hear?

In group scenarios, accountability calls for agreed-upon measurements and timeframes whereby each person, and the group as a whole, can course correct and determine effectiveness. When group members understand their roles in clear, quantifiable terms, they can work collective wonders.

CHAPTER EIGHTEEN

Reduce Drag

THE LAWS OF AERODYNAMICS govern the ease at which objects move through other matter or substances. Although there are laws that control up and down movement (weight and lift), for this discussion we'll focus on the forward and backward movement. The amount of energy we put into forward movement is called thrust. The drag or resistance an object encounters will slow the forward movement of an object and could bring it to a complete stop. Forward movement (success) is achieved when a person or organization has minimal drag and enough thrust. Eliminating drag greatly reduces the amount of thrust (or expended energy) an object, person or organization requires to propel itself forward.

Average People		Successful People
Focus on thrust		*Focus on reducing drag*

Lack of accountability creates what I believe to be one of the most self-defeating behaviors of all: drag. When you're in a conversation with another person, notice that there are usually two conversations going on. The first conversation is comprised of the actual words being spoken. I call it the primary conversation. The second conversation that occurs is one that happens inside the heads of the participants. This secondary conversation is much more influential than the one being spoken, because it's driven primarily by what we see that the other person is either missing or not telling us. It creates drag in our relationships with other people, similar to a boat that has anchors hanging over the side. It's difficult to get up to any sort of productive speed even with the motors running all out. The secondary conversation is the internal conversation wherein we fill gaps with what we know or think we know about the other person and what they are saying. It's also where we account for what we think others don't see or know.

An easy example of this is when you're talking to a car salesperson. Notice the unspoken conversation that you have in your head as the salesperson speaks. When he tells you that the car he's recommending is the best quality car in its class, you'll likely be holding another conversation in your head that says things like, "Of course he would say that; he wants to sell me the car; he wants to make a commission; he's biased toward that brand because he work for them." Although that conversation is never spoken, it packs much more of a wallop than the one being spoken. What's worse is that while we're thinking all those thoughts in the secondary conversation, for most of us the primary conversation sounds more like, "Wow; interesting; that's great". Notice how those statements don't align with what we are thinking.

I have a friend who is always looking for the next get-rich-quick scheme. He doesn't see it that way, of course. But each time I see him, he wants to get me involved in his current project or idea. He's usually passive about getting me involved, telling me about what he's doing and hoping I'll want to jump in. I usually tell him that it sounds interesting and I encourage him to let me know how it turns out. I'm already pretty sure about how it's going to turn out, but I don't want to voice it. Maybe one day he'll surprise me and actually get rich in one of his schemes, but I am predisposed, thanks to experience, to discount what he says. Once a deal goes bust or he loses interest, then he's always ready with an animated story about how he'd been done wrong by partners or whomever else he wants to blame. His unwillingness to take ownership of any of these failures further drags on our relationship, widening the divide between us and ensuring the existence of a distracting, secondary conversation.

These secondary conversations are killers. The wider the gap between what others think and actually say, the more frustrating life will seem. I'm sure my friend thinks that I'm right on the verge of investing with him even though I've never led him on. The truth is, I would immediately discount anything he said because of our history and what I perceive to be his complete lack of accountability and willingness to learn. He has created those very gaps that separate the truly successful from the "wannabe" successful. Accountability does better than any other tool I know to bridge the gaps between our primary and secondary conversations.

If my friend were to approach me and start the conversation from an accountable perspective it would definitely begin to reduce the drag in our relationship. When I don't feel like he sees what I see, then I don't feel inclined to trust the rest of what he says. Perhaps the conversation could start something like this: "Wow, I know I've gotten myself into some really bad business deals because I'm always looking for the quick buck. I'm learning, though, and I want to try something different. I don't want to keep making the same mistakes, so could I run something by you to get your take on it?" See the difference? When we feel like someone is seeing their mistakes and learning from them we are more likely to be open to hearing them directly and trusting the primary conversation.

When we front load elements we suspect will exist in the secondary conversation an interesting and much more powerful conversation can emerge. It reduces or eliminates the secondary conversation altogether. Go back to the example of the car salesperson I used earlier. Notice what happens to the secondary conversation if the salesperson were to start the conversation with a statement like this: "I want to make a sale and I want the commission from a sale and I work for Ford so I'm biased and I know a lot about cars and I picked working for Ford because I believe they make the best car on the planet." Notice what happens when the secondary conversation pieces are loaded into the primary conversation. Doesn't it feel different knowing that the other person sees their own biases? Are you more likely to be swayed with that discussion than one without loading those biases into the primary conversation?

Another friend of mine recently went to work for a large software company. The software sector he was selling in was new to him and he had a difficult time adjusting. In addition, his new VP had sliced up his territory and reduced the number of prospects he had by 70%. After nine difficult months, my friend had his first review with this new VP. It went something like this:

VP: *"Your numbers are terrible."*

My Friend: *"I know."*

VP: *"What's the problem?"*

My Friend: *"I haven't closed enough business."*

VP: *"Yes I know ... why?"*

What my friend wanted to say: *"Well, I am selling into a new software sector and just when I was making some progress, you came into the picture and sliced up my territory and now I have nothing to work with!"*

What my friend actually said: *"At the end of the day, my numbers aren't where they need to be and it has taken me longer to adapt to the territory adjustments than I expected."*

VP: *"Are you upset about the territory realignment?"*

My Friend: *"I understand that companies need to adjust territories as they grow and I believe my next quarter will show that I have made the adjustment as well."*

VP: *"I see. Where do we go from here?"*

My Friend: *"If you can go onsite with me and meet with my top three deals, I believe we can close them before the end of the year."*

Since my friend was willing to be accountable, his VP was more than willing to help him with his top deals. In the end, he closed all three of those deals, finished the year strong, and four years later, is still enjoying great success with this company.

While it was most likely true that the territory adjustments had a negative impact on my friend's performance, it was also true that there was little to gain by focusing on that circumstance. By owning his inability to produce results despite the circumstances, he was able to quickly come up with other solutions and methods of correcting the results. He was also able to get buy-in from those around him rather that alienating them with reasons and excuses.

CHAPTER NINETEEN

Three Tools to Reduce the Secondary Conversation with Other People Through Accountability

Tool 1: Verbalize what you are learning, seeing, or feeling

If we don't verbalize or disclose what we are regularly learning and experiencing, others will make their own assumptions about us. When we verbalize sincerely and are willing to stand by what we say, demonstrating that we've really learned and are committed to change, we build trust. But if we verbalize insincerely, we'll be found out soon enough, and will promote secondary conversations about us along the lines of, "he/she is all talk." When we verbalize having learned something, we put people on notice that we are changing our behavior based on what we've learned. They will be watching us to see if we really will.

Several years ago I attended a training that was designed around experiential processes. As a group, we would engage in different exercises, games, and activities, after which we would dissect what had happened. It turns out that my predisposition was to assume the role of leader in many of the activities. I was outspoken and always made sure the group heard my point. I was easily frustrated with certain people in the group and quickly decided who were the ones I thought were intelligent and worth listening to. I participated in the group much the same way I participated in life. In time, I started noticing specific behavioral patterns in myself that the group was also noticing. Some in the group were comfortable with my leadership style and skills. Most, however, were ready to deliver not-so-flattering feedback. As we recapped the activities I often heard feedback that I was arrogant, closed, unapproachable, intimidating, and thought that I was smarter than everyone else. It stung, and I initially discounted it because the group didn't really know me (which was, in fact, a rather closed and arrogant response).

By the third day of this four-day training I was seeing that I had some real problems in my behaviors and in the way others perceived them. I was seeing myself through other people's eyes (Law of Perception). I was also seeing how my behaviors were likely affecting my wife, children, and business. Initially, I wanted to explain it away, to rationalize that it was their problem if they didn't understand me. But I started seeing a deeper issue, which was that those same behaviors were preventing me from getting what I wanted out of life and in my relationships. They were keeping me from experiencing my vision. After getting clear with myself on how I was truly coming across with others, I was finally able to take ownership of my actions. What a liberating feeling.

As I returned to my office following this training, I decided to take a different approach than I previously would have. I called a company meeting with all of my employees. My normal approach would have been to tell them all the great places we were going as a company and given them a rah-rah speech. There would have been all kinds of secondary conversations going on regarding my optimism, arrogance, and self-importance. Everyone would have left the meeting verbally supportive and at the same time emotionally disconnected. Instead, I started by letting them in on what I had learned the previous four days. I said, "I've learned that I come across as arrogant and unapproachable. I also learned that I make other people feel like I think I'm smarter than them. I also realized that my optimism can get in my own way and that others perceive me as unable to see problems because of it. I probably don't see the problems all the time and that is a problem in itself. Because of how I respond to them, I create an unsafe environment for bringing up problems. I've been aloof and disconnected. And that *all changes today.* I'm committed to being a better listener. I want people to feel safe discussing issues and ideas with me. I've been doing it the other way for too long. I know it won't be easy for me, but I promise to work on it. You have my permission to call me on it when you feel like I'm being arrogant or unapproachable. Tell me what I've been missing."

Average People		Successful People
See other people perceptions as their problem		*See other people problems as my problem*

With that, I sat back and listened. It felt great. Over the next three months my little company grew from seven employees to 65. My employees doubled or tripled their productivity. My stress level dropped substantially. That meeting was a huge turning point in my business and in my life. I had similar discussions with my wife and children. As I learned to take ownership of my behaviors and how they made others feel without feeling obligated to defend or justify those same behaviors, I found a renewed sense of power and control over my life. I could tell, through others' actions, that I was being heard and understood and therefore having much more of an influence on people. Although I didn't need to change into a different person, I did need to change how I took responsibility for my own actions when I contributed to others feeling unheard or unappreciated. And as I owned my part in those feelings, I'd be willing to bet some serious money that it was easier for others to own theirs.

Tool 2: Owning and Disclaiming

Because we spend years developing certain behaviors and manners of interacting with others, it may seem challenging to make changes at all. There's a tool, though, that can help narrow secondary conversations almost immediately. It's called disclaiming. Disclaiming means letting others know that we are aware of our behavioral challenges and are taking responsibility for them. This will, in turn, impact how they account for it. As I've mentioned, some of my own personality traits include being optimistic, controlling, and analytical. Although each of those traits can be seen as strengths, they can tend to get in my own way and interfere with my relationships also.

That being the case, I might start conversations with my coworkers as follows: "So that everyone is on the same page, I'm an optimist. I've tried to take that into account as I've put together these numbers, but know that I'm an optimist." I can then proceed to outline whatever it is that I am presenting. Often people respond by saying, "I think these are pretty realistic numbers," letting me know that they don't think I've been too optimistic. If I want someone to do something my way, I might say, "I know I'm probably being a control freak, and I'd really like you to do it my way this time." Even a short disclaimer like this can go a long way toward deflating the secondary conversation about me as a control freak. We can use the same disclaimers, of course, for pessimism, anger, humor, seriousness, passion, being boring, loud, or quiet. You name it. Somehow, it's reassuring to others when they know that you see what they see and that you are doing your best to account for it. As for you, it makes you aware of your biases and will likely make you more open to other points of view. It puts the issue on the table, rather than allowing it to fester as a silent judgment in everyone's head.

Sometimes a disclaimer can simply involve owning up to a bias or agenda that you might have. If you're a salesperson, do you have a bias or agenda attached to making a sale? Of course you do. You'd rather make a sale if given a choice. Therefore, if you disclaim such a bias or agenda, you will likely be able to squelch the secondary conversation. In a sales call, you could say, "Now of course, I would really love to get the sale today, and that's one of the reasons why I'm pushing so hard. I'd also really love for you to understand the benefits of what I have to offer." A bias could be something as deep as a religious or moral belief and something as small as a color preference. By being accountable for your biases, it levels the conversational playing field and gives you more influence. Most of the time, the people you're in conversation with already know your biases. Unfortunately, unless you start by doing it for them, they will account for those biases they think you don't see by discounting or adjusting anything you say.

I have two friends about whom I had always found myself having strong secondary conversations whenever we spoke. Their religious views are polar opposites. One is an extremely conservative Christian, while the other adheres strongly to New Age philosophies. I find myself filtering anything they say through what I know to be their religious beliefs. But after engaging in a disclaimer discussion with these two, I saw that both of them had come to recognize the power that their biases have had over how they come across to other people. Neither one of them has changed their views, but they commonly start conversations with, "Now, I know I'm really conservative..." and "Now, I know I can seem pretty out there with my spiritual views..." It's funny how much more open people are with you when they know you see your own biases.

Tool 3: Be OK with Non-aligning Statements

It's important for us not to forget that accountability can often be diminished as soon as we've established it by moving on to a disqualifying statement. I've noticed that many of us learn to speak from an accountable perspective because it is less confrontational. Often we will deliver a statement from an accountable viewpoint and then turn it right back on the other person or circumstance. The most common word that completely negates accountability is "but." "I'm really sorry about my pushiness, but you sure can be sensitive." or "I know I'm an optimist, but you do have a way of bringing everyone down." Whatever comes after the "but" negates any accountability. In addition, it puts the other person on the defensive because it polarizes the emotions and feelings. The word doesn't allow for the complex feelings we often have, and forces others to either agree or disagree with us.

When we use "but," we not only deflate accountability but we also send all kinds of red flags to the person with whom we are communicating. "But" immediately renders the first part of the statement as dishonest. Normally, we use the word "but" because we think two things are mutually exclusive. All of us are accustomed to experiencing dual emotions. We can be at once concerned about poor business results yet also optimistic. We can be angry and frustrated yet loving and caring. We can be excited and skeptical all at the same time. We really can. The problem arises when we frame these dualities with the word "but," because it instantly disqualifies one of them. And usually the one it disqualifies is the one that listeners would like to hear an accounting for. One who is trying to be persuasive is less likely to say, "I think my high projections are realistic, but I'm an optimist," as opposed to, "I know I'm an optimist, but I do think my high projections are realistic."

The solution to this is simple: convert the word "but" to the word "and." It doesn't discount one side of the statement. "I love you and I'm really frustrated with you right now." "I know I'm an optimist and I really think these high projections are realistic." Notice how "and" doesn't diminish or reduce the accountable statement. Notice too how it makes it OK to have complex or mixed feelings without dismissing one of them.

As we account for our own feelings and biases and recognize our predisposed tendencies, we can also better account for how others arrive at their conclusions. Our very ability, in itself, to account for our flaws becomes the underlying foundation of accountability. Many of us are willing to assume something is a fact without accounting for how we arrive at those facts. The mere process of accounting for how we reach certain conclusions creates room for us to explore alternate possibilities and perspectives. Rather than just say I believe my political beliefs are accurate, I have a slightly different perspective when I account for how I arrived at my political beliefs. "My parents raised me to have conservative (liberal, moderate) political views which I've adapted over time to my current political views." This by nature creates some tolerance for others being taught politics by their parents and arriving at different conclusions than mine. It removes my political views from the fact category and puts them in a slightly different category that allows others to come to their own conclusion without diminishing my passionate beliefs.

Finally, accountability is a crucial backdrop for learning. If we place blame or focus on something outside of us, there is nothing to learn. Even when we blame ourselves, we learn nothing. But when we are willing to look objectively at the processes, beliefs and decisions that have led us toward a specific success or failure, we open ourselves up to an ever-increasing number of opportunities to learn and, inevitably, succeed.

Applying the Law of Accountability

These questions may illuminate areas where you can better apply the law of accountability in situations where your results are less than optimal:

What was my contribution to the outcome? Remember that not contributing can also be a contribution to an outcome. Likewise, playing a minimal role or playing too big of a role might contribute to an outcome.

What did I feel that I ignored or didn't say to anyone?

Was I clear on the expected results? Did I ask clarifying questions or did I make assumptions? Did I communicate clearly with others?

Did I ignore information along the way that pointed to the eventual result?

How did I handle the result?

What have I learned, and what can I do differently next time so that this result doesn't repeat itself? Be careful with this question. If your answer is "I learned that I can't trust anyone else to do things," or "I learned who my real friends are" then you aren't being accountable. Notice how those statements place blame on others and really don't provide any meaningful insights toward how you can do something different. Look at these statements of learning instead: "I learned that I haven't inspired others to give 100%," or, "I overestimate the value I've created in my friendships." Can you see the difference between those two statements and the previous ones? Learning means that you've not only identified what doesn't work, but also that you've identified at least one course of action that might work better.

When we get a result that is what we wanted or expected then we might ask the following questions:

What did I contribute to this working result?

What did I learn so that I can continue that behavior in the future?

How can I do even better next time?

Again, accountability is a way of being. Initially it takes practice and we turn it on and off as we become aware of opportunities to be accountable. Eventually it becomes part of who we are. As we are accountable, we will find that others around us also start to be accountable. Being surrounded by accountable people further pushes us toward being accountable.

Challenge: Take an event or experience you've had that, up until now, felt completely beyond your control. Notice the story that you've created around that event. Retell it to yourself without any blame, including not blaming yourself. Start with decisions you made prior to, and subsequent to, that event. Include decisions that others made, but don't assign any other intentions or assumptions about those decisions. End the story by finding at least two things you could learn from the experience (that are about you and not about others).

THE FIFTH LAW
THE LAW OF
LEADERSHIP

CHAPTER TWENTY

The Law of Leadership (Harness the IQ of Others)

TRUE LEADERSHIP IS THE PROCESS of leveraging the people around us to create maximum value. Once we've applied the first four Laws—Vision, Frequency, Perception, and Accountability—then Leadership takes over to determine how far and how big we can go. From my perspective, leadership refers to the ability to take ordinary individuals and transform them into a brilliant group. Brilliant groups distinguish themselves by adhering to a larger, collective consciousness. This is different from mere conglomerations of brilliant individuals, which are liable to struggle with leadership. In this book, great leadership has two important attributes: aggregation and diversification. Aggregation refers to the process of listening and becoming smarter because of the insights of the group. Diversification means to consciously expand the group with broad and diverse insights, experiences, and approaches rather than making groups homogenous.

In 1860, a little-known backwoods lawyer from Springfield, Illinois decided to run for President of the United States. He had run multiple times for national public office, but had only been elected to a single two-year term in the U.S. Congress. The Republican Party had arisen only four years earlier from the remains of the Whig party and was still sorting out its leadership. At the time, the country was in turmoil, with several southern states threatening to secede from the Union.

Abraham Lincoln felt like he could unite the country. That year there were three other stronger candidates who sought the nomination, including William Seward, a prominent senator from New York State, along with Edward Bates and Salmon P. Chase, the popular governors of Missouri and Ohio, respectively. Although the Republican convention of 1860 took place in Illinois, Lincoln would nonetheless struggle to win even his home state's votes. Because the other candidates were so strong, they split the first ballot with no one getting the required majority. Lincoln won on the second ballot because none of the supporters of the three stronger candidates wanted to support another strong candidate.

After such a stunning upset, Lincoln struggled to win the support of the losing candidates. They had seen him as having no chance of winning, and appeared more than willing to go on record with disparaging remarks. According to Lincoln biographers Nicolay and Hay, Chase, in particular, was unable to open his mouth or pick up a pen without "speaking slightingly of the President."

The national election saw Lincoln pitted against the Democratic candidate Stephen A. Douglas. After a long, bitter election cycle Abraham Lincoln ended up winning with 32%—the smallest plurality in history. He had lukewarm support from those who voted for him, and staunch opposition from the 68% who had voted against him. It was arguably one of the most difficult election scenarios in the history of the United States. What happened next is what defined Lincoln as a true leader.

Lincoln's first task as the President Elect was to assemble his cabinet. It was customary at the time, as it is now, to give key posts to those who were instrumental in your election. Lincoln had made no such promises to his supporters. Instead, he started with his three nomination rivals and offered them key positions in his cabinet. For Bates, Seward, and Chase, these represented huge steps down from their current political posts, and each of them demonstrated their lack of respect for Lincoln by promptly turning him down. Lincoln nonetheless proceeded to court them with his unique leadership approach. When told by his opponents and adversaries that they disagreed with his politics, Lincoln responded that it was for that very reason that he wanted them as advisors. He looked for those who could see things differently than he did.

Next, Lincoln reached across the aisle to the Democratic leadership and offered them positions as advisors and cabinet members. Years earlier, Lincoln had been hired as an attorney in a large antitrust case in Ohio. It was a huge case, the pinnacle of his legal career. Shortly after Lincoln had been hired, another attorney was also brought onto the case. His name was Edwin Stanton, and he was at once brilliant and self-important. He also had Lincoln promptly fired, refusing to work with someone to whom he referred as a "third-rate, backwoods attorney." Notwithstanding this humiliation, which had sent Lincoln into deep depression at the time, Lincoln offered the prominent and crucial position of Secretary of War to none other than Edwin Stanton, who of course turned him down.

Through Lincoln's persistent efforts, each of those rivals eventually did agree to be on Lincoln's cabinet. They were all outspoken and Lincoln did little to rein them in. Instead, he relished the different insights that each brought and regularly sought their input and advice on decisions both large and small.

One story that puts Lincoln's leadership style into focus had to do with an appropriation for the War Department, which Lincoln had approved. When a representative approached Stanton to collect the funds, Stanton, who thought the appropriation was ill conceived, turned him away. When told that Lincoln had personally signed the appropriation, Stanton replied that Lincoln was a "damn fool" for approving the appropriation and refused funding. The petitioner went back to Lincoln, hoping to get enforcement for the approved appropriation. Lincoln, who was puzzled by Stanton's refusal to pay, asked the gentleman what Stanton had said. "Stanton said you're a damn fool," the man had replied, expecting to harden Lincoln's resolve. "Is that exactly what he said?" Lincoln asked. After hearing the man's affirmation, Lincoln replied, "Edwin Stanton is the smartest man I know. If he said I'm a damn fool then I probably am. I need to reconsider this appropriation."

What a leader. Can you imagine the President of United States being that open to learning from his advisors? Lincoln's willingness to hear all sides and incorporate those opinions into his own decisions have played no small role in securing Lincoln's popular perception as perhaps the greatest President the United States has ever seen. He didn't achieve his success through intellect alone, even though he was extremely bright. He managed to aggregate multiple viewpoints and to gain insights based on a variety of opinions. This didn't characterize Lincoln as weak or indecisive. Many times he would make decisions that ran contrary to what his advisors had strongly recommended. He would, however, regularly shape his ideas through the input of those he respected because they saw things differently.

Average People		Successful People
Surround themselves with like-minded and like-skilled individuals		*Surround themselves with diversity and opposing views*

Leadership is all about aggregating IQ. It is about leveraging the people around us to make our own decisions smarter and at the same time, to get "buy-in" from those who have contributed to the process, even if the ultimate decision doesn't come down in their favor. Not only did Lincoln do this, he was also able to exercise and master a most powerful element of leadership: listening.

Listening, as opposed to merely hearing, is usually handled one of two different ways. The first is listening with the intention of rebutting, and it's probably one of the most common approaches. Whenever I catch myself listening this way, I'm barely even hearing or understanding the speaker's point of view because I'm so preoccupied with formulating my next response for when they stop talking. This form of listening and leadership inevitably produces poor decisions, resentment, and a lack of buy-in from those around you.

The second, more effective way of listening is done with the intention of being influenced. When listening this way, we are earnestly seeking another's point of view. We actually want to hear something that will change how we see or feel about an issue. As Lincoln understood, if we can learn to see or feel things differently, then we'll likely be able to make better-informed decisions. Often we can incorporate someone else's insight entirely and not only get all that we wanted, but also address the other person's concerns.

Great leaders reach outside of their group. Using politics as the example, there is a huge difference between the political leaders who have managed to polarize a party and the ones who have reached beyond their own party and brought the insight, talents, and solutions from diverse and opposing views. It's one thing to preach to the choir, get your employee base excited, convince your existing customers that their purchase decision was a good one, or enroll your spouse or children in something. Not to diminish from the importance of getting those who already believe the same as you on board, but there is a much higher level of leadership. Getting those with already similar views as you doesn't have that much of an impact since, after all, they already agree. Transformation in life, business, and relationships occurs when you can get those who don't or didn't see it your way to engage in your vision. Sometimes that means expanding your vision.

CHAPTER TWENTY-ONE

The Human Dilemma

I'VE NOTICED SOMETHING INTERESTING as I've worked with people across broad backgrounds. In a group setting, most tend to see themselves as being smarter and more insightful than the people around them. Business owners will typically see themselves as being the most intelligent in their group—after all, they're the owners. When I interview other members of the management team, however, most feel the same about their intelligence and abilities, feeling that they understand much of what the owner doesn't. The first question I ask employees in these interviews is always the same: "If you owned this company, what would you change or do different?" A phenomenon then occurs in which everyone throughout the organization—all the way down to the janitor—see their own solutions and ideas as being absolutely guaranteed to work better.

I see the same thing going with couples and friendships, as well as between parents and children. Both sides think they possess some extraordinary insight that the other one lacks. I'll illustrate this point using circles to represent our individual "IQ." In this section, I use the term "IQ" loosely in reference to the consolidation of our intelligence, skills, talents, abilities, insights, experiences, knowledge and wisdom—the whole of what we can contribute in life. I'll assign a number on a similar scale as traditional IQ to illustrate how we generally see ourselves in relationship with others. Most of us, like those high school students in Section 3, see ourselves as being significantly smarter than those around us. In this case, the high number of 130 will represent you (with the largest circle), while the others will be assigned numbers 110 and 90 respectively, symbolizing those you might know who are relatively smart (110) and those who you consider to be not very smart at all (90).

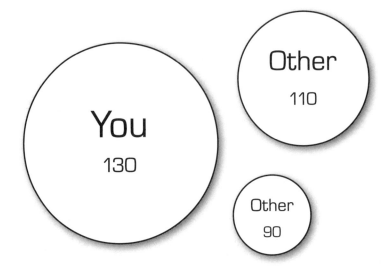

In this case, our assessments of everyone's abilities—including our own—aren't as significant to our leadership issues as are the ways in which we see the circles combined. Compare the circles depicted above with the ones depicted below:

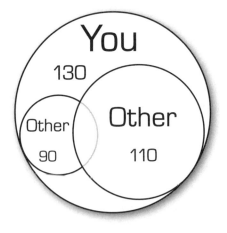

What does this second illustration suggest about the relationship between you and these other two people? Since both of the other's circles are inside your circle it suggests that you know everything they know, and then some. Unfortunately, it's often how we treat others. If we were managing these people according to the point of view represented by the second diagram, how would we treat them? If one of these people was my spouse or child how would we treat him or her? According to the diagram, we would treat other people as objects that we needed to direct and impart upon our vast and all encompassing wisdom. There would be little use in asking them for input, or even requiring us to listen, for that matter, other than as a gratuitous effort toward making them feel good. What's more, the collective intelligence of the group would be limited by our intelligence. The total possible intelligence of this group would remain at 130 (our intelligence).

Have you ever found yourself viewing a situation this way? Do any of us have all of the insights, knowledge, experience, wisdom and skills of any other person on the planet? Of course not! How can we say we've had the same exact experiences as any other person? Instead, a more accurate diagram might look something like this (even giving ourselves the benefit of having the biggest circle):

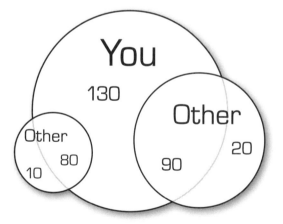

Examine for a second the possibilities represented by this third diagram. What does it say about the IQ of the group? For one, it means that the potential IQ of the group would be 160, if we can pick up the IQ points that fall outside of our own circle. While the difference between a 100 IQ and 110 IQ isn't really that much, the difference between 130 IQ and 160 IQ is extraordinary. Even though this opportunity to pool our resources is available to us in all human interaction, why do we resist capitalizing on the collective IQ that surrounds us? Most achieve whatever success they experience in life based primarily on their own efforts and hard work. Those who can effectively harness the power of the group achieve much higher levels of success.

Let's explore this group dynamic a bit more. A group can consist of a couple, a family, friends, business associates, employees, or any combination of those people. I've established something I call a Brain Trust in several areas of my life. I use the term Brain Trust, even though many of the groups might be better described as a Heart Trust. I rely on them a lot for feelings, spiritual insights, and non-intellectual contributions. I have different groups I draw on for personal issues, business issues, family issues, financial issues, and so on. Some of them are formal, established groups with formal relationships; others are simply people I respect and trust. Most of us already have groups like this in our lives—it's of utmost importance that we also take full advantage of their ability to contribute to our own IQ.

CHAPTER TWENTY-TWO

Creating an Effective Brain Trust

MANY YEARS AGO I started the first small business that I owned completely. I was only 25 years old when I started Brett Harward Consulting. (I was very creative when selecting a name for my company.) My company provided custom computer programming services for businesses. Soon enough, I was able to hire a couple of other programmers and a receptionist, and my business was off and running. I was the senior programmer, sales person, administrative staff, and any other role that needed to be filled. I excelled at programming, and felt that it was my primary asset and competitive advantage as a business owner. I was much weaker at marketing, sales, finance, HR, and many of the other core business areas.

Once the company had taken off, I considered bringing on a partner who could help me facilitate my desire for expansion. I interviewed several potential partners with various backgrounds and technical abilities. My decision came down to two people: one was an excellent programmer who had run the IT department for a large developer; the second had more of an accounting background. Even though I desperately lacked financial and accounting skills, I was turned off by my perceived image of "geeky" accounting types (meaning anyone who had more pencils in their pocket protectors than me). So naturally, I fell in love with and hired the programmer immediately, because I considered him to be like me. Since I saw myself as a smart and good businessman, I felt that others who were like me would also be great assets to my business. This programmer and I had so much in common (such as the ability to have entire conversations in acronyms) that we got along great. We rarely disagreed. We were excellent at the technical aspects of what we did. We applied our technical abilities to solve any sort of business problem. For example, our approach to increasing sales was to make our program work so well and have so many features that people would beat our door down with no relative sales effort on our part. (That's how technicians generally approach sales.) Our approach to marketing was to describe our technical features completely, starting with those that were most difficult to program. Our company continued to grow, even with our lopsided management team.

When the time came to bring on another person, I found another brilliant programmer. Using our circle diagram I was creating a group that looked something like this.

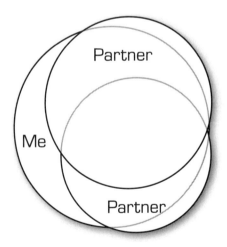

Notice that when I form a Brain Trust of like-minded, like-skilled people, the opportunity for aggregating IQ goes down dramatically. Not only did the skill set match, the personalities were also similar: optimistic, innovative, not detail-oriented. You can imagine the types of things we could talk ourselves into. We always felt like we were right on the cusp of remarkable success, that we were merely a few features away from programming ourselves into riches. Needless to say, my company's fatal shortcomings pointed directly toward my unwillingness to bring forward—and benefit from—a wider variety of insights and approaches, particularly from those dreaded areas of accounting, sales, and marketing I'd so avidly resisted.

I see people make this mistake over and over again. I work with many in the building industry and noticed this interesting parallel. The builders who had risen through the ranks wearing a tool bag would most likely surround themselves with a management team that came from a field labor background. The builders who had an academic entry into the building profession were likewise more likely to hire someone from the local college construction management program to fill a management opening. Both groups would duplicate themselves over and over again. Most of these companies were unsurprisingly weak in the other, equally crucial, areas of their company. The individuals I work with often surround themselves with those that share similar skills, income, hobbies, and personality types. Granted, this is an approach that's hard to resist because it feels effortless. We don't have to work very hard to appreciate and tolerate those who we see as being like ourselves. We are naturally much more open to input that comes from those who we consider to be like us. And of course, they'll probably agree with you the vast majority of the time.

In my case, I would regularly seek out other optimists to bounce my business ideas off of. We would start with a million-dollar idea and by the time we finished our optimistic one-upsmanship, we would have a multi-billion-dollar idea on our hands with little or no changes to the original idea's substance. Discussions about downside risks and threats never entered into the equation. We wanted no pessimists raining on our optimists' parade. I've since grown to greatly value having pessimists (or "realists" as they usually like to call themselves) as part of my Brain Trusts. I've got enough optimism that it takes a room full of pessimists to offset it—and I need it. As I listen to them with the intention of being influenced, I've found that they have extremely valuable insights.

Likewise, pessimists would be well served to have an optimist's input. As we learn to identify our realistic strengths and tendencies and surround ourselves with those who would challenge those tendencies, our decisions and collective intelligence will improve. Some areas worth incorporating into our own Brain Trusts might also include those who are innovators, detail-oriented, systems-savvy, relationship-driven, sales-minded, introverted, extroverted, intuitive, analytical, creative, or results-oriented. Those are just a few, but since most of us tend to overestimate our own strengths and underestimate our weaknesses, anything outside our own personality and skill set is worth considering.

Average People		Successful People
Prefer being the teacher		*Love being the student*

I once took a test that measured people's tendencies toward being innovation or execution-oriented. The maximum score on either side was 130 points. Most people who took the test scored somewhere between the two areas with a slight favor toward one of those two traits. I took the test, and wasn't surprised when I scored 130 on the innovation side of the equation, knowing that I'm traditionally strong on imagination and weak on details. One of my partners took the same test and not surprisingly scored 130 on the more detail-oriented execution side of the equation. Although we can drive each other nuts, we make great partners and we completely respect what the other person brings to the relationship. And our third partner brings a completely different set of skills to the mix. She adds an objectivity and results focus that is refreshing and keeps us on track when the other two of us get hung up on the emotions and relationships in a given situation. All three are valid views and prove much more insightful when combined. We rarely have the same approach to anything. We often disagree, but we can foresee problems and innovate solutions in ways I was never able to see in earlier decision groups. And to have it any other way is a frightening thought.

CHAPTER TWENTY-THREE

The Power of Aggregating IQ

T HE MOST ACCURATE PREDICTOR of future events is, believe it or not, gambling. When gamblers place bets on horse races or sports events, they are essentially expressing their opinions of likely outcomes. Thus, if a horse goes off at a 3-to-1 long shot, it will statistically win almost exactly 25% of the time. Professional sports betting will hit the over/under almost exactly 50% of the time. The realistic odds in betting owe their accuracy to the aggregated true IQ of the masses. Because people are betting real money, they are compelled to state how they really feel without the rhetoric that is likely to seep in when there's less at stake.

The University of Iowa established a betting forum for people to bet on political futures called the Iowa Electronic Markets (IEM). In one study, the IEM compared its betting results with the results of 964 polls conducted during the presidential elections from 1988 through 2004. The IEM (betting) outperformed polls 74% of the time, and outperformed the polls 100% of the time when forecasting more than 100 days in advance. It was significantly more accurate in long-term forecasting than polls because those who participated had something tangible at stake that increased their honesty. And when more people participate by betting, the closer the odds will predict the statistical probability of an outcome. The largest form of legalized gambling in the world is the stock market. It's incredibly predictive of future performance. Stocks will often adjust for market interruptions before the interruption even occurs. Like with betting, this is a result of aggregated IQ.

In some of the training sessions I conduct, I demonstrate how this works using a jar of jellybeans. As I begin speaking I will start a large jar of jellybeans circulating throughout the room. Each participant will be asked to guess the number of jellybeans in the jar. We raise the stakes by telling them there will be valuable prizes for the winner (the entire jar of jelly beans, in fact). Some do careful mathematical calculations counting the jellybeans along the bottom and sides of the jar. Some estimate according to how many bags of jellybeans they think might fit in the jar. Some go off of their gut feeling. Others make wild, off-the-mark guesses. Whichever methods the participants use to arrive at their numbers, one statistic remains constant: over 90% of the time, the group average is closer than any individual's guess in the group. And when someone has managed to beat the group average, it's almost always a fluke that's unlikely to repeat itself over multiple tests.

The group IQ is always greater than any individual IQ in the group. Let's go back to the circle diagram:

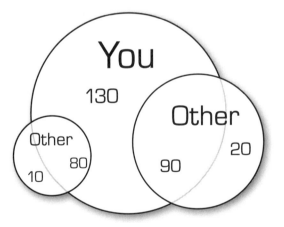

Look at those areas where "what you know" and "what other people know" overlap. This is, of course, where you'll find easy agreement. This is also the area where we are likely to respond that we already know something, in case those who are making the suggestions get the false impression that they've shed new light. Usually, when we uncover something we didn't know, thanks to someone else (the part outside of your circle), we will not immediately recognize it as valuable. All too frequently, we feel the urge to initially reject the idea because it comes from outside of our circle of knowledge. We don't know what we don't know. Great leaders understand this, and as second nature, pick up extra IQ points by aggregating their group IQ.

I refer to groups that limit their IQ according to the smartest (or not smartest) person in the group as "Little Smart." They fail to take advantage of the IQ points that are lying around waiting to be picked up.

Little Smart groups and organizations have the following traits:

- Decisions are made with little input from others.

- Conflict and disagreement are considered "bad."

- Teams are exclusive. ["We have enough information already," or "You're not qualified," might be their catchphrases.]

- Decision groups are like-minded and like-skilled.

- Most decisions are seen as either/or.

- Expert status is heavily weighted.

Groups that can capture the IQ of the group, where each individual is looking for the IQ points that others offer, is called "Big Smart." Big Smart groups and organizations have the following traits:

- Group input is welcomed, sought out, and encouraged.

- Conflicts and disagreements are seen as "IQ moments."

- Teams are inclusive.

- They seek diversity.

- Most decisions are seen as and/if.

- Non-experts are respected.

Furthermore, Big Smart and Little Smart individuals are distinguished by the following criteria:

Little Smart	Big Smart
Assume that others don't see the big picture or are missing something.	Assume I don't see the big picture or am missing something.
Assume that silence means someone has nothing to say.	Assume that silence might mean that others are waiting to be asked.
Listen with the intention of rebutting or defending.	Listen with the intention of being influenced.
Avoid discussing key decisions with those around them.	Seek input from others regularly as part of learning.
Avoid discussions which might produce conflict or disagreement.	View disagreement and conflict as gifts.
Rely on compromise and consensus	Find the third dimension of solutions when possible.

The first difference outlined in this table is life-changing. When we hit points of contention, disagreement, or confusion we can start with one of two assumptions. We can assume that the other person or group is missing something, or we can assume that the disagreement signifies that we're missing something. When we approach it from the standpoint that we're missing something—instead of that the other person is missing something—we listen better, we learn more, and we often discover that we were, as a matter of fact, missing something. And in the cases when we listen to people and hear them exploring issues we may have already considered, it's actually a good opportunity for us to verify that the conclusions we'd already arrived at are sound.

Average People		**Successful People**
Often see others as competition and adversaries		*Always look for ways to have others be allies*

CHAPTER TWENTY-FOUR

Six Indicators of Potential IQ Points

I SEE IQ POINTS AS THESE LITTLE (or big) pieces of intelligence scattered all around us that we can either bend over and pick up, or pass by because we feel we already have enough. Picking them up takes effort, including a willingness to have our egos bruised. But when we weigh our visions against the possibility of an occasionally bruised ego, the best choice should seem obvious to us. I have compiled a list of moments, based on personal experience, when you might consider paying special attention because they're the moments that are certain to offer up IQ points. If you incorporate these into your management style and relationships, you'll notice a guaranteed difference.

We are likely to gain IQ points when:

1. We find ourselves challenged, criticized or defensive. This is the time when most people shut down and close themselves off. So often we think it's more important to be right than it is to get it right. We think our circle is sufficiently large to handle the situation. That being so, we might find ourselves saying, "It's not your call," or, "Don't tell me what to do." Instead, when we find ourselves feeling challenged or defensive, we can recognize it as an opportunity to pick up some IQ points. Defensiveness is a surefire indication that we're running the risk of missing out on important information or opportunities to improve. What's more, it tells people that they better not be honest with us because to do otherwise would be too unsafe. We therefore train them to bite their tongue or even lie to us. If we encourage honesty and contribution, and behave as though we mean it, they'll respond accordingly, and we ultimately won't regret it.

2. We find ourselves significantly outvoted on an issue. As the primary owner of several businesses, I often have the opportunity to meet with minority partners. It creates conflict sometimes because the voting entitlement isn't the same as the number of people who are voting. In other words, if I own 90% of the company and have two partners, then my 90% outvotes the other two people who own 10%. There's generally a reason that I own 90% of the business and I have a responsibility to act in what I feel is the best interest of the company. Having said that, I have red flags that go up when I get significantly outvoted on an issue. I've found that this means I'm probably making a mistake or that I'm not seeing the complete picture. At those times when I proceed with a decision even after being outvoted, I need to make certain that I've checked my ego at the door.

3. Only one person sees it differently than we do. Once I was on a Board of Directors for a certain non-profit group. Even though those on the board were good friends of mine, the board was divided into two well-defined groups. And for my purposes, let's refer to them as the "business people — those who held the leadership positions, were relatively wealthy, and did most of the talking — and the "BBQ planners" — those who mostly took care of events, put together phone trees, and rarely offered input at our meetings. You might guess that I was in the business group, and the BBQ planners probably would have labeled the groups differently than I did. They might have referred to us as the "Big Ego" group or the "rich group". I'm exaggerating the divide between the two groups for purposes of this illustration, although there was certainly a real gap at our board meetings.

During one of our meetings, someone proposed a fundraising activity for an outside group. We didn't have a lot of details about this group, but they wanted to use our non-profit organization to raise tax-exempt money from donors and then funnel it back out to their community project. We would get publicity out of the deal. After a couple of minutes of discussion the 13 of us that were present voted on the proposed project. The vote was 12 to 1 in favor of allowing this outside group to use our non-profit organization for fundraising. The one dissenting vote came from the "BBQ planner" side of the group. My instinct was to barrel ahead since no one on that side of the board, surely, had enough business experience or expertise to truly impact our decision.

However, I'd been working on this rule, and the single dissenting voter, who hadn't spoken, aroused my curiosity. I stopped the discussion for a second and said to the dissenting voter, "I must be missing something. Why would you vote against this?" She replied, "We've spent a lot of money to keep our non-profit in good standing and I don't think we know enough about this project and its use of funds to approve this right now. I don't want to jeopardize our non-profit status." I was dumbfounded; she had a great point. We re-voted on the issue and decided to suspend the decision by a 13–0 vote. I later hired her as a consultant for my company. She was way more than a BBQ planner.

4. We don't want to discuss a decision with anyone else. Sometimes we find ourselves hiding decisions from others. While some decisions should be confidential, it's tempting for us to keep things under wraps that we know won't stand up to challenge. When we catch ourselves not wanting to tell anyone about a decision, that decision becomes highly suspect.

I decided to hire a new employee once for a key position in my company. I was initially surprised when I received so much push-back from those around me. My partners were concerned about the hire. My wife was really concerned about the hire. Several people told me that in private, this person was very critical of me and my company, and that what he said in management meetings was completely different than what he was saying outside the meetings when I wasn't there. When challenged I would typically respond with, "It's not your call," or, "I'm not asking for your opinion on this one." The criticisms were coming at me from every angle, so I decided to be covert about my plans to expand the role of this person, because I didn't feel it was worth going through the push-back from the others on my team. I justified my decisions by telling myself that I was a better judge of character than those around me. To justify by resistance to my partners feedback I told myself that they were judgmental and jealous about a new person coming into an important position in our company. My refusal to engage or even tell others about my decisions regarding this person only made matters worse. I saw the decision as my prerogative and my call despite its impact on those around me and the negative effect on the general morale of my organization. I was more concerned about not being wrong, even as evidence had already started to suggest that I had made a mistake. I dug my heals in deeper and became more committed to my stand. As you can guess, it eventually became apparent that the decision was one of the worst hiring decisions I had ever made.

5. We find ourselves avoiding talking about a decision or course of action with certain people. When we find ourselves only wanting to discuss a decision with like-minded people, we'd better be careful. On the contrary, we should go out of our way to discuss ideas with those who will likely not agree. Their input is invaluable.

As I began writing this book I found myself having to work on this one. I wanted others to read it who had already demonstrated that they bought into its contents. I wanted people to agree that it was a great concept and brilliant tool and looked for those people, bypassing those who I thought might not "get it." As I recognized what I was doing I began making a conscious effort to get input from those who I felt might not like it or who subscribed to different ideologies than I did. It turns out that those people gave me my best feedback. They caused me to explore in greater depth some of what I was teaching. They questioned many of the premises that I held as self-evident and caused me to find examples and stories that would better illustrate the points I wanted to make. As you read this book, you are the recipient and benefactor of much of their feedback.

6. We feel like another person has nothing to teach us. Every day we have opportunities to pre-judge people and deem them incapable of bringing anything of value into our lives. We can size them up according to health, age, income, or appearance. We throw out the baby with the bathwater when we do this. I've learned some gems about business from some of the most unsuccessful clients I've had. I've learned some powerful lessons about caring for others and loving others from the criminals who have attended seminars I've taught.

Anytime you find yourself writing someone off as not having something to offer, be very suspicious of your motives. Everyone has IQ points they can offer at some point. Those who are constantly looking for opportunities to pick up IQ points end up being far smarter than even the brightest of those who go it alone. After all, a veritable sea of humanity stretches out between each of us and our vision. We may as well dive in.

Applying the Law of Leadership

To see areas where you might be able to apply the Law of Leadership, consider the following questions:

Who do I regularly involve in my important decisions? What do I see as their purpose when I involve them? Do I see the purpose of others as endorsing or agreeing with my decision or do I want to know and hear what they really think? I have one friend who starts me laughing each time he calls. The conversation usually goes something like this: "I'm thinking of working with this company and we're putting together a contract. I'm thinking about structuring it like this. What do you think?" When I say, "I would shorten the timeframe, tie it to results, and make sure and spell out expectations," I already know his response. He will say, "I like having a long time" or, "we don't really know what results we want yet." To which I will say, "Great, it sounds like you've got it under control," and when I hang up the phone I feel like it was a complete waste of time. When this person calls I now know that what he wants me to say is that his idea sounds great. From my perspective, though, I don't even care if he agrees with me or decides to take my advice. All he would have to say is "Great input" and I would consider our conversations to be worthwhile.

Who do I avoid when making important decisions?

When I make mistakes what are the tendencies that have become patterns? What are my "isms" (optimism, pessimism, pacifism, fanaticism, victimism, fatalism, etc.)? Who do I know that can compensate for my personal "isms"?

Challenge: Take one current issue or area where you would like to increase your insights. This could be in a relationship, finances, spirituality, health, or some other area. Find two people with whom you can discuss the issue or area. The first person is to be someone you expect will have similar views as you. The second will be someone who you guess will have opposing views. You are to leave your ideas out of the discussion. The purpose of the conversation is only to tap into any insights the other person has. For example, if you chose spiritual, the first person might be someone who has very similar spiritual beliefs while the second might be a minister, priest, monk, or member of a completely different sect, faith, or belief system. Your job in both conversations is to listen and understand fully what the other person sees. Notice which conversation produces more insights. How were your views expanded from the conversations?

CHAPTER TWENTY-FIVE

Applying the 5 Laws:
Newton's Second Law of Motion

I N SECTION 1 WE DISCUSSED Newton's First Law of Motion, which states that objects at rest will stay at rest, while objects in motion will stay in motion at the same speed and direction, unless acted upon by an unbalanced force. We saw how it applies to people, organizations, and groups much in the same way it applies to objects. The 5 Laws you've read about in this book — the progressive series of steps that work together to change and improve life's outcomes — corroborate Newton. His Second Law, in fact, works as another particularly useful illustration for how the 5 Laws can work together for our benefit. This law is the equation F=MA, or force equals mass times acceleration. To restate this law as it might apply to people, force could be synonymous with impact, influence, or success.

How do we affect force by mass and acceleration? We can build mass by incorporating the insights — and accumulating buy-in and support — from others. High levels of success require the mass value that only comes from having others supporting us. As I worded it previously, a "sea of humanity" lies between our visions and us. This includes our significant relationships, children, families, coworkers, friends, communities, governments, customers, vendors, and many others who can either join us in moving toward our vision or block us at every turn. Becoming Big Smart, eliminating drag, and increasing our Value Quotient can kick-start the process of increasing mass in our lives.

As we build mass (as in "masses" of people), we must also build acceleration, i.e., Frequency, by establishing measurements, letting go of moldy peanuts, embracing feedback and getting over the need to be right. When combined together, mass (people support) and acceleration (Frequency) have an exponential impact on each other, with one multiplying the effect of the other. This combination of the two makes for the fastest and most efficient way of achieving our desired outcomes in life. Below I've outlined a series of additional questions that might illuminate areas where the 5 Laws can be applied to gain mass and acceleration, thus bringing your vision to reality.

The Law of Vision

What is the outcome I want from this situation, relationship, or area of my life?

If you can't completely answer that, then ask yourself these questions:

What information or resources am I missing that would make my vision or desired outcome clearer? How could I get that information?

The Law of Frequency

What indicators would tell me I'm on track with my vision? How will I feel when I achieve my vision?

*What are some possible starting points or methods I could use to move me toward my vision? What can I do **today**?*

As soon as you see three or four ways to achieve an objective, then the possibilities and creativity can begin to flow. If you lock yourself down to one way, then you inevitably exclude too many people and possibilities. Get in the habit of seeing options not only in what you can do about something, but how you could feel about something. One great exercise is to come up with an option and then list the exact opposite as another option. For example, if you're feeling controlled or invalidated, you might look at the same circumstance you're in and consider whether the possibility exists that you're actually being loved and appreciated. When my wife reminds me to slow down when I'm driving, she may well be doing it because she thinks I'm stupid and a lousy driver. Most likely, though, she cares deeply about me and doesn't want something bad to happen.

You could have the most expensive product on the market, or you could have the least expensive product. Whatever the case may be, you will make better decisions if you consider all options. Here are some more questions to ask yourself:

What are five, 10, or 20 strategies, tactics or mechanics that might work to achieve the result I want?

How will I measure whether I'm on track or not? If I'm not on track, then what will I do?

The Law of Perception

How can I get input from others to let me know how I'm doing and where I could improve?

How can I quantify the feedback I get?

Who can I involve in my Brain Trust?

Who am I resistant to talking to about my vision or being part of my Brain Trust? How could I benefit if they were involved? What insight might they contribute?

What do others see in me that might get in my way?

The Law of Accountability

What can I do to own and account for that which prevents me from having what I want?

What people or circumstances do I blame for my lack of success, and how can I see those issues from an accountable perspective?

Why haven't I achieved my vision yet? What parts of me would likely need to change in order for me to be the person that achieves the vision I have?

Who do I see who is currently reaching levels I'd like to reach? What can I learn from them?

The Law of Leadership

Who else could contribute to my vision or the possible paths to my vision?

How can I involve them?

What are some tendencies I have that create repeated biases or blind spots?

What types of people would offset my personal tendencies and who do I know would fill some of those slots in my personal Brain Trust?

To apply the 5 Laws in your career, here are some questions you might ask yourself:

Where would I like to be in five years?

What are three strategies that could get me there?

What additional information would I need in order to get where I want to be with my career? How could I get that information?

What additional skills would I need in order to be where I want to be? How could I get those skills?

Who would need to be enrolled or brought in for me to get where I want to be in five years?

Who can I share my vision with verbally so that they can hold me accountable to achieving my vision?

What will be the indicators along the way that tell me I'm on track? What are the timing targets and how will I measure my progress? What are the financial measurements that will indicate the value I'm creating and the track I'm on?

What is it that my coworkers, managers, and subordinates want from me? How do I create Maximum Value for them? (Don't guess or assume. Ask them and give them choices.)

What are my personal behaviors, skills, abilities, or ways of being that others might perceive as being in my way? How do I compensate for, embrace, correct, or adjust those behaviors?

What has stood in my way up to this point (be accountable!) that has prevented me from achieving my goals? How did I allow or create the current result I am experiencing?

Who would support me in my goals, vision and objectives? How can I incorporate their insights into my forward movement?

How can I own what's gotten in my way in the past and let others know that I see it?

What can I change in order to get better results?

Do I have a personal purpose statement?

Here's an example of how someone's application of the 5 Laws might look:

Right now I'm an administrative assistant. The vision I have for myself is to become a Director-level manager in the marketing department of my current company in five years. My benchmarks to make sure I'm on track include the following: Becoming a team leader within 12 months of today's date; to be a department supervisor within 24 months; and, by December 31st, to go from my current $16/hour to $24/hour. The ways that I will increase my value by at least 50% will include a much higher focus on my end results. My communication skills are weak and I tend to throw up my hands when I hit a roadblock. I'm committed to be more patient; I'm also going to take a communication class that my manager recommended within 30 days. I'm not sure of the exact skills that the company looks for in a Director. I will make it a point to talk to at least two directors in the next two days to gather their insights on what I would need to do to improve skills and chances of becoming a Director. I know I am weak in finance and numbers and that in order to be a Director I need to understand and use numbers better than I do. I'll take an accounting class next semester at the local community college so that I have a better handle on numbers. I'll register before Friday at noon.

Others tend to see me as shy, negative, detail-oriented, and needing lots of management. I've even heard myself described as arrogant and aloof, and can see how someone could read that into how I treat others. I'm committed to working on being a better communicator, being solution-oriented, persistent, and getting the ball in the end zone. I'm not sure about other things that people might see as being in my way. I'm committed to asking five people this week so that I have a better handle on what I'm dealing with. I am putting together a Brain Trust that will help me compensate for my tendencies that get in my way. Bill will be in my brain trust specifically to add an element of optimism, and I'm committed to at least try and see his optimistic point of view to offset my tendency to see the negative. I'll give him permission to call me on my pessimism so that I'm at least aware of it. Lisa will also be part of my brain trust to add an important element of innovation, since I tend to get stuck in the details. I'm committed to check in monthly with my direct report at work and get a numeric rating on how I'm doing. My target is to gets 9s or better on a 1-to-10 scale and I'm committed to change things immediately if I'm getting lower scores. I'm working on not blaming others when I don't get the job done, and instead focusing on my contributions to results achieved by me or my team.

In the short term I want to create sufficient value so that I can get a raise to $18/hour within 3 months. I also want to shift positions from administrative assistant to more of a front-line, hands-on role within 60 days, or sooner if a position opens up. I will let my supervisor and others know where I would like to go and ask for their input and support. I am also working on trusting others, and teamwork skills.

If this were your starting point, the trajectory of your career would change dramatically. Look at all the opportunities available for learning, growth, change, and seeing things differently than before. The more you course correct, gather feedback, and reassess what you're doing, the greater the likelihood is that you'll stay on track and achieve your vision. This approach also gives you a sense of maturity and objectivity that is so highly sought after in today's business environment.

As a business owner or manager the 5 Laws could be applied as follows:

Do I have a company (department/division) vision (mission/purpose statement)?

Does the vision statement contain a clear specific purpose that contextualizes the company rather than focusing merely on what the company does? (Compare "Our purpose is to give voice to ordinary people," with "Our purpose is to be the leader in self-published books." The first is much more powerful and expansive, the second more vague and restrictive.)

Do I have a written business plan that defines the objectives, exit strategy, strengths, weaknesses, opportunities and threats that play a role in how successful I am? (I suggest a strong focus on weaknesses and threats, since seeing them will cause the most significant changes and improvements in the business. I use a 90/10 ratio focusing 90% of my business plan on weaknesses and threats and only 10% on the strengths and opportunities.)

Who should I share my vision and business plan with? (Partners, managers, employees, bankers, vendors, advisors, customers, spouse.) Have I shared my vision and plan with them?

Can I describe my vision in a way that expresses clearly what I want? How could people who hear me support me if they so desired?

What are the objectives and benchmarks that will tell me I'm on track with my vision?

What are my financial revenue and profitability targets daily, monthly, annually, and five years from now? How can I get that information accurately and frequently so that I can course correct when I'm not on track?

What other benchmarks will be good indicators of whether or not I'm on track? (Offices, locations, employees, market penetration, productivity, customer satisfaction, turn-around time, customers, awards, etc. — remember to establish measurement and date for any benchmark.)

What are activities or events that would be predictive of "bottom-of-the-funnel" results? (Phone calls, leads, demonstrations, testing, units produced, quality, networking, follow-up, contacts, alliances, etc.) How can I manage predictive activities on an hourly, daily, or weekly basis?

What do I do when I find myself off track? Who else should I involve? Have others bought into the targets I am shooting for?

Do I have a financial plan or model (budget) that supports my business plan and my organizational structure? Do I use it regularly? Do I hold myself accountable to my overall targets?

Do I have a flash report that gives me my key indicators for my business or department? Do I get it daily or at least weekly?

Is there a formal structure in place to receive feedback from employees, coworkers, subordinates and managers?

Have I defined the customers of my department or company? Do I ask them what they want and where I should be focusing my resources and efforts? Is there a formal structure in place to handle customer feedback?

Do I regularly use and share the feedback I receive? Am I resistant to the feedback I receive?

Do I provide clear messages describing benefits to customers and employees for working with us?

Do I humanize my customers and employees or do I treat them as objects that can contribute to or interfere with my success?

Have I spelled out expectations in writing and in processes so that customers and employees know the expectations from association with my business or department?

Do I practice writing down policies and procedures in order to eliminate making the same mistakes over and over? Do people follow and learn from the policies, procedures, and processes that I've established?

Do employees have clear position guides, job descriptions, and performance measurements that will accurately and objectively reflect how they are doing in their job without subjective assessment? Is performance measured frequently against clear performance expectations?

Is subjective assessment regularly given?

Do my coworkers, subordinates, and employees feel valued and heard? Do they feel like they make a difference?

Do I express gratitude regularly to employees and coworkers?

Are employees and coworkers offered training to enhance their skills and abilities and to provide them with tools for personal and business growth?

Do I conduct frequent employee reviews as a consistent process in the business? Are the reviews forward-moving and quantifiable? Do the employees participate by sharing their insights, frustrations, goals, and recommendations in that process?

Are employees regularly rewarded for contributions and improvements that have a positive impact on the company as a whole?

Is the sales process designed to identify what consumers value? Am I doing most of the talking or are they? Is the customer experience consistent in both the sales and operational aspects of the business?

Do I measure customer satisfaction? Employee satisfaction?

Is there a culture of honesty with employees and customers so that they always know where they stand?

Have the roles of customers and employees been defined and communicated in a way that holds them accountable to their roles?

Does management look for diversity and differing opinions?

Is there a plan to compensate for weaknesses in skills and behaviors with the management team? As I add additional employees, am I aware of the skills, views, or insights that will add to the existing team rather than having significant overlap?

Have I identified my tendencies and proactively sought out managers and outside people who can offset my behavioral tendencies and at least give me opposing viewpoints?

When you hit a problem, dispute or roadblock you can use the 5 Laws as a guide for forward movement.

1. **Vision:** What is your vision?

2. **Frequency:** How can you tell if you're on track? What do you do if you're not on track?

3. **Perception:** Who else can give you perspective about how you're doing?

4. **Accountability:** What actions or results can you hold yourself accountable for?

5. **Leadership:** What are the resources, information, and people around you that you're not currently using effectively?

Epilogue

AT THE AGE OF 32, THOMAS MIKO BAYNES had already achieved considerable success. He was happily married, and had two young children who were his pride and joy. Even at his relatively young age, Thomas had developed a mature, well-adjusted worldview that stood out among his friends. When he was 19, Thomas had started working on his own. Initially he had cleaned up construction sites in the evening after his regular job managing a local fast-food joint. Within a year he had several regular contractors that used his services and he hired some of his friends to assist him in cleaning up the job sites.

Thomas hadn't started out with many financial advantages to speak of. He was determined, however, to reach a level of financial independence that would enable him to explore the world a bit. Although he wasn't certain how he would reach this goal at the time he started his modest cleanup service, he was fascinated as he spoke to the general contractors and foremen on the jobs he worked. He listened intently as they described their problems with waste, theft, and efficiency losses that resulted from the poor management of job sites. Before long an idea started taking shape.

Over a decade after Thomas began, he owned over 1,500 portable on-site storage units and over 600 dumpsters. He had built a company with a reputation for excellence and a long waiting list for his services. He had found a unique niche in his local market and was meeting a need that had gone largely unnoticed. But his business didn't always flourish.

His optimism almost left him bankrupt when he overextended himself on his first purchases of cargo containers. Fortunately, after a period of trial and error that he watched over closely, he was able to learn quickly from his mistakes. He had remedied his lack of financial experience by bringing in a partner that had a better financial background than he did. He had gone on to assemble a great team of managers and employees that he could trust to run the company as he formulated his next move. He had married his beautiful wife in his mid-twenties, and especially because they were both willing to make major adjustments in various behaviors, their marriage was now stronger than ever. They had both matured quickly in the ways they dealt with each other and worked together on their marriage.

Now, Thomas found himself on the last leg of a long vacation. He had traveled throughout Europe with his family for the first portion of the trip, but had a personal pilgrimage he wanted to make for the tail end. Thomas had always wanted to visit his ancestral homeland deep in the heart of Uganda. He wanted to connect in some way with the people and places he'd heard stories about as a child—stories that had been passed down from generation to generation. What hit Thomas hardest when he first arrived in Uganda were the seemingly endless scenes of poverty and hardship he witnessed. At first, his heart sank in despair over the experience, only to find solace in his admiration for the spirit, strength and even humor of the Ugandan people. Thomas was aware of the country's troubled past, filled with war, corruption, and political unrest. He was also aware of promising signs that pointed to potential political and economic recovery.

Thomas had spent the first part of his visit to Uganda by exploring the mountainous jungles and rainforests so prevalent throughout the western part of his ancestral home. Now he found himself near a savanna which stood in stark contrast to the mountainous forest regions he had visited only days before. He knelt down by what must have been an ancient watering hole. It made a striking impression on Thomas. Although it wasn't especially large, being only a few meters across, the crystal clear water seemed to emerge from nowhere along the base of three giant granite stones.

As Thomas sat in the silence of the morning his mind wandered back and forth between his ancestors and the Ugandans of today. He wondered what life had taught his forbearers, and if those lessons would have any applicability to their present day posterity, so many of them living in desperate conditions. Most of all, the question, "How can I help?" echoed throughout his mind. And as he sat where a wise ancestor of his did generations before, waiting patiently for the emergence of wild game, Thomas experienced something similar. He had captured himself a new vision.